Wine Country In Shorts

The Stories of Napa & Sonoma

Ralph De Amicis & Lahni De Amicis

Cuore Libre Publishing

Napa California

Wine Tasting In Shorts
The Stories of Napa & Sonoma
By Ralph De Amicis & Lahni De Amicis

Published by Cuore Libre Publishing
Napa, California
www.WineCountryInShortscom

Maps: Ralph De Amicis
Photos Lahni DeAmicis & Ralph DeAmicis

Pg 16. San Carolos entering San Francisco Bay by By Walter Francis - Public Domain

Pg 148. Stage Coach GG Joh Y. Nelson - Public Domain

Contents

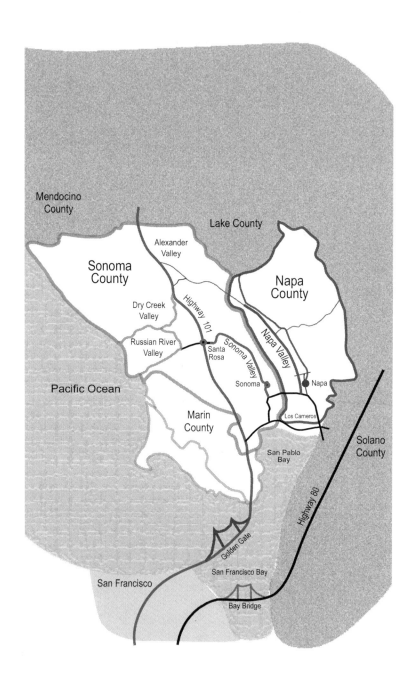

Chapter One
Wine Country, A Land of Stories

These are the stories that I've told to clients thousands of times while driving them around Napa and Sonoma. I (Ralph) recall the tales best when we visit the places where they happened, so to create the stories for this book, I dictated them into my phone, *while my clients were tasting at the wineries* in those regions. In between the stories are short chapters with my answers to the many questions We've been asked about what makes this region so unique. A wine region's personality is not just about the topography and climate, but also about how the people living there adapted to its unique qualities. Those 'answers' add context and texture that make the stories more relatable, because whether we realize it or not, we are all shaped by our natural surroundings.

We've (Lahni & Ralph) wanted to record these stories for a while, but it was hard to find the time. And then a fortuitous thing happened. The local wine tasting fees escalated, and the wineries recognized that if they abandoned their quick tasting bars, in favor of longer seated experiences, their sales improved. Honestly, *any tour guide could have told them that!* The big wines grown in the North Bay vineyards taste better the longer they are allowed to open in the glass.

That scheduling change suddenly gave me a predicable amount of precious, uninterrupted time to dictate the stories, and then later improve the drafts. I have an essential partner in Lahni, who manages our client appointments from the office. She also edited and improved the stories, not only correcting the spelling of the names and checking the historical facts, but always adding 'the fun.'

While I do occasionally arrange last-minute winery visits when I'm on the road, unlike many guides, I'm spared having to juggle constant customer calls in between driving. In the early years I used that free time for onsite research for our tour books, but now I was able to use it to assemble these stories.

It still amazes me how many stories pop out of my mouth as we drive around with clients. Sometimes I remember them because they relate to a friend at a winery who first shared it with me. Or when we're traveling through the place that is the backdrop for that drama or comedy. *Many stories have been around so long that there are multiple versions.* For instance, four different people are credited with naming Mount Saint Helena, the beautiful volcanic cone that towers over Napa Valley. But, if you keep an open mind, dig deep enough into the research, and account for human nature, you can weave the various versions together into an enjoyable, credible narrative that's pretty close to the truth.

For me, *this reweaving happened spontaneously through telling the stories* numerous times while noticing both my listeners responses, and whether or not it 'felt' true as I spoke the words. That is a concept from the healing arts, because hearing lies makes us weaker, while hearing the truth makes us stronger!

Even though the stories give us the big picture, the descriptions of the traditions and practices in the winemaking world seem to be endlessly interesting to our clients. Two hundred years ago most people worked on the land. Today a tiny fraction of Americans grows everyone else's food and wine, so for most people, this life on the land is far removed from their personal universe. There must be some deep region within us *that still yearns for that ancestral connection to nature.*

Is it due to our ancestry, our genetics, or simply our sensual enjoyment of wine, that so many people are drawn to visit the places where it's made? I think the answer to that is 'Yes,' to all of the above! Winemaking is a very elegant type of agriculture that has delightful results. Visiting Wine Country is an adventure, although not as risky as it was in the early 1800's when visitors had to contend with the numerous California grizzly bears that lived here. I think that's why bravery and audacity are so prized locally, and why this region attracts so many of the big personalities who show up in these stories from the past and present.

We're sure a scientific study would show that wine tastes better when accompanied by a story, and any story becomes more enjoyable when the wine is good.

Any experienced winery host knows that's true, which is why, as they fill the glasses, the best share stories about the winery's history and location. There's only so much you can say about what's in the glass, because to our bodies, flavor is a language, and great wines have no problem speaking for themselves.

When they tell the story of the struggles involved in clearing the land, planting the vines, building the winery and making a good wine, that connects the guest to that bottle in an emotionally memorable way. Later, when the guest opens the bottle at home, that memory makes the wine taste 'better,' and they have the added pleasure of telling that story to their friends and family. So, I feel that the best way to enjoy these stories is with a glass of wine in your hand. If you are listening to this as an audio book while driving in a car, we'll give you a pass on that.

On the road I've shared these tales with clients in *15 to 20-minute snippets*, which is the ideal driving time between wineries, because it allows enough time to metabolize some of the wine in preparation for another tasting. But here I've combined those pieces into complete stories, and many turned out to be much longer than I expected. The stories span the wine regions of both Sonoma and Napa, and yes, the two are delightfully different.

I think of historic Sonoma as the older sister, a good-looking girl, a wonderful cook, hard working in the house and the garden, content with her family and long-time friends. She likes things the way they are and doesn't want them to change. While Napa is her younger, golden-haired brother, who shares a few of her best qualities, but not her humility. He's always curious about visitors and technology from afar and endlessly looking towards the horizons. Whenever little 'Napa' walks into the room, everyone stops and makes a fuss. *While 'Sonoma' resents all that attention her little brother gets, 'Napa' adores his big sister,* buying grapes from her Pinot vineyards and always saying wonderful things about her.

The more often you visit the two of them, the less likely you're able to choose a favorite. Because the first seven chapters are about the early history of the region, Sonoma plays a bigger role in the stories.

This book is a celebration of *the unique storytelling style that goes well with wine:* colorful, relaxed, thoughtful, a little rambling and segmented. That's because the pace of the story allows time for the listeners to taste the wines and enjoy the illumination it bestows. That's how the ancients described the experience of drinking alcohol, 'being illuminated by the wine.' We hope that you enjoy these stories that are only as remarkable as the wonderful places and people they describe, and that are treasured by so many.

Lahni's Editor Note: The Northern California Wine Country is peppered with similar and overlapping stories, many from slightly different perspectives, so you will find that some of the details are repeated, often with a twist that reveals a bit more about the bigger story. So, feel free to dip into the book at any chapter and know that the repetition is intentional, and you will also be better prepared for the Quiz at the end of the book.

(Just kidding, or are we?)

The Historic Toscana Hotel, Sonoma Plaza
Opposite: Golden Gate looking Southwest

Chapter Two
The Mysterious Golden Gate

For visitors coming to California who are trying to understand its unique nature, it helps to realize that Spain and Mexico controlled a string of influential settlements in this expansive region for hundreds of years. That explains its laid-back nature, especially in the southern part where Spain reigned the longest. *Northern California is different.* When you cross the Golden Gate Bridge from San Francisco and drive towards Sonoma and Napa, you're venturing into the northern tip of where the Spanish empire once stretched in the Americas.

During that early colonial period, Spain was a major power and their territories included Florida, half of south America, Central America, Mexico and the

American southwest. Eventually, they reached this far north but no further, leaving a trail of towns with Spanish names; San Diego, Los Angeles, Santa Barbara, Santa Cruz and pretty much 'Saint Everybody Else.' They completed their city naming spree at the top of the Sonoma Valley with a city named for the first Saint from the Americas, Santa Rosa de Lima.

The road that connected their California Missions together was *the 'Camino Real,' or 'Royal Road.'* It wound north from Guatemala, then to Mexico City through the rugged interior. It follows ancient Aztec and Rio Grande Pueblo tribal foot trails to New Mexico, and then west to the Pacific Coast. There the Franciscans established the first California Mission named for 'San Diego' and over the years worked their way north. El Camino Royal was the original Main Street in many California towns, including the little city of Sonoma, *where it ends at their Plaza* and the final Franciscan Mission, 'San Francisco Solano.'

In California the ancient road has been marked with a series of bells on top of shepherd's crooks. Being the site of one of the twenty-one missions is the gold standard for qualification as an historic site. The second tier goes to the Spanish forts, or Presidios for which San Francisco's famous army base was named.

Finally, the third criterion belongs to the six Spanish Pueblos, the cities where courts were convened, and official records kept. The surprisingly small city of *Sonoma is the only place in California that enjoyed all three of these distinctions*, albeit for the shortest period of time.

But I'm getting ahead of myself, so let's go back to where so much of the North Bay's story begins, the Golden Gate Pass at the entrance to the San Francisco Bay. It sits midway up the coast of California, and *it's cunningly hidden from the seaward side*. Since the mid-fifteen hundreds Spanish galleons had sailed past the strait unaware, on the way back from their bases in the Philippines six thousand sea miles to the west.

After a five-month journey returning from the spice islands, they would make landfall along the Northern California coast. After taking on fresh water, and whatever other supplies they could find, they would turn south towards their base in Acapulco. *They sailed well off the coast* to avoid the submerged dangers along the rocky shore. They named their various landings along the coast including Point Mendocino, Bodega Bay and Tomales Bay.

Western historians often neglect to mention that the Portuguese and Spanish first successfully ventured into those distant seas *using charts created by Chinese cartographers* who had come before them. In the early 1400's, during the Ming Dynasty, the Yongle Emperor dispatched seven fleets of Chinese 'Treasure ships' to map the world. Those grand ships were *twice the size* of the largest Spanish Galleons, and they were accompanied by smaller Korean and Japanese trading vessels.

Fortunately for the Spanish, one of the fleets meticulously mapped the Pacific coastlines of North and south America, including Magellan's passage, which provided easier access between the Atlantic and the Pacific Oceans. They also mapped what we know today as the San Francisco Bay.

However, when ships sail into unknown waters there are always shipwrecks, which explains why early Spanish explorers *reported seeing Chinese junks sailing along the coast in the 1500's*. The Spanish sailors recognized the design of the Chinese trading junks from their travels in the Western Pacific and the Indian Ocean. There were so many sightings that the Spanish concluded that there must be a Chinese city nearby. They called this place they never found *Quivira*, after Francisco Vasquez de Coronado's 'Seven Cities of Gold.'

Even though it is possible that those ships were recent arrivals, more than likely, they were repaired and sailed by the shipwrights and sailors that had been left behind when the fleet sailed home in the mid-1400's. That's not surprising, because unlike European ships, the Chinese crews included both men and women, so between shipwrecks and the inevitable babies, there were more people in the fleet than berths on the remaining ships.

There is plenty of genetic evidence that Chinese communities from the fleets remained behind in the Americas. As they watched the ships sail away, they surely expected them to return. *Sorry!* By the time the fleets made home port the Yongle Emperor had died. His xenophobic son, appalled at the massive expense of the fleets, systematically closed the borders and put an end to their mapping and exploring. The new Emperor and the influential Mandarins closed China off from the rest of the world for the next four hundred years. *As an interesting footnote* of that decision, a California State anthropologist found a village of 'Indians' in the Russian River Valley in the 1800s *who only spoke Chinese.* The next time a Chinese ship would enter the Golden Gate Pass was in 1850, bringing immigrants into San Francisco Harbor.

Even though the Chinese withdrew into their 'Middle Kingdom,' they left behind the world maps created by their fleet cartographers in places like Kolkata (Calcutta), a trading port the Chinese had established in earlier sea going days on the coast of India. It was there that Venetian navigators found the charts and brought them home to 'La Serenissima,' their beloved Venice. The charts helped Venice expand into a major sea power.

Their rise did not go unnoticed and led to a heavily disguised Prince Henry of Portugal smuggling the charts out of Venice to the Iberian Peninsula. Those precious charts were the keys to prosperity for his country, and if he had been caught, he would not have survived. Henry set up a sailing school on the Portugeuse coast to train crews to use those maps.

Today, on its site, a statue of *'Prince Henry the Navigator'* looks out over the ocean. With the help of the Chinese charts, he developed a sea route to the spice islands. They avoided the dangerous Venetians and Arabians, by going around the tip of Africa. In a shockingly brief period of time Portugal went from being Europe's poorest country to its wealthiest.

Eventually, the Spanish and English, through captured ships, obtained those charts, and Magellan used one to find his passage to the Pacific. Sir Francis Drake depended on them *when he circumnavigated the globe* in the late 1570's, landing north of modern San Francisco, on a section of coastline that he claimed for England. This was a serious puzzle for Captain Drake because the Chinese charts showed a great bay along this part of the coast. The Spanish had sailed these shores for years but failed to find its location. Drake surely wanted to claim that prize for himself as it would make his fortune. But just because the chart said it was there, that didn't make it easy to find.

The Spanish Ship San Carolos

From our perspective today it's hard to imagine what those navigators contended with. We are accustomed to seeing the shoreline from the decks of cruise ships, a hundred feet above the water, or looking down at where the land meets the water while flying above the Earth in airplanes. During Drake's time, the first flights of the Wright Brothers were hundreds of years in the future. What you could see from the low deck of a bobbing ship, was what you knew. While the San Francisco Bay is expansive, its sole opening to the sea is a narrow strait, barely a mile wide *and it hides in plain sight*. At the time when Drake was tramping along the coast, impenetrable marshlands lined much of the shoreline that fronted steep cliffs.

For a sailor looking eastward from the sea the view is deceptive, because beyond that narrow opening are both Alcatraz Island, one of modern San Francisco's most popular destinations, and Angel Island, the *'Ellis Island of the west.'* Then beyond those two grassy mounts are the green hills of Berkeley. Their various heights conspire to make the pass appear as a solid wall of rocks and vegetation meeting the churning sea.

Then to complicate a ship pilot's life, there are the famous fog banks that blanket the area for many months of the year, making the coastline appear and disappear like a magician's rabbit. As if that wasn't enough to dissuade mariners from venturing closer, California's two largest rivers empty into the ocean through the Golden Gate. The turbulence that pours out of that narrow opening is epic, filled with whirlpools and eddies that can swallow a small boat.

The only reason there aren't more wrecks sitting on the bottom surrounding the harbor, like we see at ports around the world, is because so few ships could find their way there in the first place. Because those two rivers carry nutrients from magnificently fertile countryside, the waters offshore are packed with life. That makes the shallows around the nearby Farallon Islands the perfect breeding ground for one of the ocean's great alpha predators, the absolutely *terrifying great white shark.*

So, let's see if we've got this straight. When the sailors passed that part of the rocky coast in their little wooden ships, what they saw was *fog enshrouded, tumultuous, shark infested waters* that any smart, experienced Captain would avoid. It's amazing that the Chinese found the entrance in the 1400's, and we know that they did because there's wreckage from their ebony ships buried under the silt of the Sacramento River a hundred miles upstream.

When the Spanish arrived at the Sacramento Delta in the 1700's, the local 'Indians' were farming rice in those fertile lowlands, a plant that traces its origins to the banks of China's Yangtze River, now known as the Chang Jiang. Even today, you can see the squat and ridiculously cute rice silos dotting the local fields. The advantage that the Chinese cartographers enjoyed aboard their spacious ships were stables for horses. They could easily ride along the coast with their instruments, taking their sightings and making their notations.

The Golden Gate could not stay hidden forever from the European navigators once they had the Chinese charts, *but still it eluded them from the seaward side.* How did they find it? The story has been told for generations by the Bay Area families of the twenty-one Spanish soldiers who walked thirty miles north from Half Moon Bay and practically fell into the watery inlet. The Franciscan monk in charge had ordered them to reach Point Reyes, a pointy spit of beach, jutting out into the ocean thirty miles north of the Golden Gate Pass. That's *where Drake had landed two hundred years before* and curiously, Point Reyes sits right on the troublesome San Andreas fault line where two tectonic plates come together. The party made their way north and came to the wall of marshlands that once ringed the bay. So, they headed inland, probably because the coastal route was so cold. As they traveled inland, they encountered a violent band of braves that *aggressively charged their party*, keeping up their attacks until the soldiers fearfully turned back. Hoping for a safer route, the party walked towards the coast and up the peninsula into what is today modern San Francisco.

They were making satisfactory progress until their way was blocked by the tumultuous, deep waters of an inlet. Being soldiers and not sailors *they deemed the route to Point Reyes impassable without a boat.* As simple soldiers they had never seen the Chinese charts drawn three centuries before. Such things were only for trusted navigators.

They didn't realize *they had just discovered* the entrance to one of the world's great bays, something that had evaded European explorers for two centuries. Feeling defeated at not reaching their destination, they returned to Half Moon Bay. They apologetically explained to the Franciscan Monk how they failed to reach their destination, due to the marshes, the devilish Indians and the 'unexpected body of water that touched the sea.'

Despite the significance of their find, it was several more years before enough of the threads were pulled together that the Spanish navigators could match the shoreline from the Chinese charts with the reports of this expedition. Finally, in 1775, the unlikely Spanish supply ship, 'San Carolos', with a *young, inexperienced Captain*, found the entrance to the harbor. He had been promoted at the last minute because his Captain went crazy just before weighing anchor at Monterey. Possibly his youth led him to be more daring and willing to venture where the previous captains had feared to tread.

First, he cautiously sent a rowboat though the pass. When his mate reported back that it was clear they sailed the ship through the treacherous waters, finally mooring off Angel Island in Ayala Cove, *named for the courageous young Captain*. It's located just below a steep slice of land called Tiburon, which not surprisingly means 'shark.' Obviously, the sleek gray predators that patrolled the strait's entrance impressed them.

That was before freighters and steel warships plied these waters and encouraged the natural world to give them a wider berth. Over the next two months, the pilots used the longboats to map the bay's expanse. Captain Ayala and his men befriended the mostly naked local tribes, who envied their warm coats. Even though they marveled at this amazing discovery, they had yet to see the Eden-like valleys to the north.

It's accepted that the favorite place to moor boats is along the steep Sausalito shore, where you'll find all shapes and sizes of craft, including *the town's eccentric and colorful houseboats*. The town's location on the leeward side of the Marin headlands shields it from the cool Pacific breezes, so when the fog wraps around the headlands, it leaves a patch of blue sky above the town. Many a time I have sat in the local cafés, sipping a coffee while watching the fog flow between the high-rises across the bay.

While the Chinese Treasure fleets were long gone by the time the Spanish appeared along the coast, *many other countries have raised their flags over California.* The stickiest problem was Sir Francis Drake's claim. The Spanish clearly controlled the area south of the bay, with a prominent Presidio in Monterey. That's where the future commandant of Sonoma, Mariano Guadalupe Vallejo was born.

Even though it was years since Drake had raised the English flag over Point Reyes and Bodega Bay, *the English had never relinquished the claim,* and that posed a problem for the Russian Governor of Alaska. He needed a warm coastal settlement where his people could grow food to support his fishing bases.

The Russian Governor was wary of infringing on the powerful and quite testy Spanish, so he consulted with their leader. he felt he could conveniently ignore Drake's previous claim, because this was the ends of the Earth. So, he sent a ship south to establish what is commonly called Fort Ross. Although pronounced 'Fort Ross,' it was named for 'Mat' Rossiya,' or Mother Russia. Their settlement was just north of where the shoal choked Russian River empties into the Pacific, and it gave them a warm, fertile place to farm and raise animals. In a delicate bit of diplomacy, they avoided the lovely natural harbor at

Bodega Bay, claimed by Drake, but named by the Spanish. Instead, they chose a spot along the steep, wooded coast just north of the *unnavigable Russian River,* because no other seagoing power would be interested in wrenching such a marginal ship's landing from their grip.

The success of this settlement caused some serious stress for the Spanish who had Presidios in Monterey and on the shores of the San Francisco Bay. In an aggressive geopolitical chess move, now Lieutenant Vallejo was sent from Monterey to establish *a Presidio* north *of the bay and closer to the Russians.*

The spot he chose became the little city of Sonoma, the most historic place in California. His mandate was to prevent the 'Russian Bear's' influence from spreading to the south, which was a problem because *the Russians were well-liked by the locals.* Also, Vallejo was a genial man who was happy to have a good relationship with them and really didn't have enough soldiers to make it an issue.

Eventually, when the Americans arrived in greater numbers, the Russians abandoned their 'fort,' it had cannons but no soldiers. The Czar was afraid that his people would become *'infected with democracy.'* So yes, it was good old Russian paranoia that made them leave Paradise, although not all of them did.

There are still old Russian families in that part of the Redwood Empire, as it's traditionally known, and in San Francisco, once again, thanks to the Golden Gate. After the Czar of Russia fell from power, aristocrats fled the country, and a favorite route was from their westernmost port, Vladivostok, to the Golden Gate and San Francisco. Not surprisingly, *they settled in an area called 'Russian Hill.'* This steep, picturesque neighborhood was named for an early colonial cemetery, the final resting place for Russian fur trappers who were hunting the precious sea otters, and occasionally coming to an unfortunate end.

The Russian Aristocrats were an entirely different breed from the early trappers because they arrived with their gold and jewelry, which they put in the city's banks. The story goes that so much wealth left 'Mother Rossiya' in those émigré's trunks, that the Russians paid informants working in the oldest banks. They were to watch for members of the old Russian families accessing their safe deposit boxes from that period. This commercial espionage went on until the fall of the Soviet Union.

The Golden Gate has consistently been the source of the city's wealth. At the time of the Gold Rush, thousands of miners arrived on their way to the Sierra Madres. Then t*he gold flowed* through those banks and back out the Gate on ships. Even that didn't compare to the wealth from the Nevada silver mines which arrived in the city's banks and firmly established it as a financial powerhouse. All of this prosperity is in addition to the vast amount of agricultural wealth that passes through the Gate, *and not just from the wine.*

Which brings us back around to poor Sir Francis Drake. He had unknowingly suffered a bit of bad luck. *For the lack of a good walk* of about ten miles down the coast from Point Reyes, he missed finding the entrance to the San Francisco Bay. With its great natural harbors and navigable rivers, it is the envy of the world. If Drake returned today, from his landfall at Point Reyes, he could ride east on Sir Francis Drake Boulevard to Route 101, once called the Redwood Highway. Then he could follow 101 south over the Golden Gate Bridge to San Francisco's Union Square.

After an appreciative glance at the statue of the beautiful Uma Spreckels, high atop her towering podium, he could march into the Sir Francis Drake Hotel and demand a suite. I'm sure they would be happy to accommodate him, since they owe him a small fortune in royalties for using his name for so many years.

Admittedly, there has been talk of renaming that boulevard, because while his ships sailed under the English Flag, the Jolly Roger would have been equally appropriate. We must remember that sailors once compared this part of the coastline to the pirate infested Barbary Coast of Africa, so Drake would feel right at home as he looked out from his suite over the busy square, *as he raided the minibar. Argh!*

Chapter Three
The Gift of Mustard

Most visitors come to Wine Country in the warmer weather, with peak season happening during harvest in the late Summer through early Fall. It's a festive time of year when the vines are heavy with fruit and the scent of crushed grapes fills the air. We often explain to clients that they'll rarely see grapes being picked because that normally takes place in the coolness of night, under tractor mounted lights, for the sake of both the grape's freshness and the worker's comfort. But, if they're up and out early, they'll see the fruit laden trucks arriving at the crush pads at dawn, when the winemakers take over.

Fewer people visit during the cooler off-season. They're mostly the Canadian snowbirds and collectors, who are anxious to taste the vintages released in the

Spring, and happy for fewer tourists on the roads and in the wineries. At that time of year, the vines are dormant, the bushy canopies of leaves have been blown away by the Winter winds, and the workers are pruning away last year's canes. The *vineyards are transformed* into tight rows of woody vines, revealing their simple, orderly geometry. But the visitors are rewarded for their off-season travel with a delightful floral display. Bright yellow bands of wild mustard flowers appear like magic carpet runners, laid down between the bare grapevines. The yellow blooms add a touch of sunshine to the vineyards during our Winter rainy season.

They are a unique signature of Winter in the North Bay Wine Country when the rains transform the bleached, golden hillsides to a verdant green, making it the favorite season for many locals. While many trees keep their leaves, the deciduous trees go bare making the statuesque evergreens stand out. As the views open up they offer peeks of the spectacular hillside homes and wineries that are normally hidden by Summer's leafy privacy screens.

I've often joked that in Summer this region looks like *Tuscany* while in Winter, it looks like *Ireland*, if only the Irish grew grapes instead of shamrocks. Of course, with climate change, the way the English are currently growing sparkling wine grapes, it's less of a joke than I once thought. What's remarkable for people from outside the area is how quickly the look of the place changes. From the moment when the first rains arrive, a lush groundcover springs up between the bare vines. You can practically watch it grow, and very quickly it's followed by the tiny yellow mustard flowers, appearing like stars emerging from a darkening sky.

But *Wine Country is farm country*, albeit with great restaurants, so the cover crops the vintners choose for the wet Winter hiatus depends upon the needs of the land. A primary consideration is helping the bare ground stand up to Winter's wind and rain. It's important to keep the dirt securely in place around the roots to discourage both disease and industrious gophers. Next the choice depends on what nutrients the vines need. If they have a hankering for nitrogen, they may plant some type of bean, to capture that element from the air and bind it into its roots.

When the springtime plow comes through, the mineral will be released into the soil by the blades. Once or twice, I've seen vineyards with stripes of red clover flowers, but that deep pink bud is more commonly used as a cover for other crops. Mustard and wild radish's talent for inhibiting problematic insects makes them a popular choices.

Ground covers also serve other purposes. When a vineyard finally runs out of steam and the vines are ripped out, the vintners will begin the lengthy process of preparing the land for the new vines. If they want to lighten heavy clay soil, they'll plant the herb, borage. I've often seen those tall spindles reaching up from recently cleared ground near the river, aware that they are digging even more deeply into the clay. Just once I saw a fallow vineyard *planted with spectacular sunflowers,* but that was a special time. The longtime owner of the vineyard, a native of Kansas, had passed away so the family had planted that state's official flower in a glorious tribute for everyone to see.

Not surprisingly, the farmers are happy when a helpful groundcover comes up by itself with the rain, saving them the work and expense of planting. That's one of the talents of the very prolific wild mustard, making it the area's most popular Winter cover. We often see it growing wild by the side of the road and in abandoned meadows. But often, farmers plant it in time for the Winter rains because it's rich in phosphorus, which gives grapes a strong, thick skin, and produces spectacular colors in the wine.

Flavors live in the skin and the more they can encourage that healthy layer with bright sunshine, the tastier the resulting wines will be. That's why you'll see workers removing the leaves that are shading the bunches but leaving the ones on the other side that protect them from the wind.

The wild mustard flowers are so widespread in the North Bay Wine Country that locals watch for their annual appearance and passing as an indicator of the changing seasons. At the peak of its season, it's common to see lines of cars on the weekend pulled up alongside especially abundant fields, as visitors stream out with their cameras to capture that brilliance. The blooming mustard is so much a part of our daily lives that most people would be surprised to find out that *it's not a native plant*, quite the contrary.

Even though mustard plants are found throughout the world, the bright little yellow flowers were first brought here by the Franciscan Monks in the 1800s. Historically, trailblazers always carried items for trade, because there's nothing like exotic gifts to open the doors of potentially unfriendly locals, like the beads and bangles infamously used to purchase Manhattan.

Mustard is a valuable plant, for both its medicinal and culinary qualities. The pungent flavors must have been *a wonderful surprise* to the native people and its ability to stimulate healing warmth and sweats could be lifesaving.

Today it's hard to imagine the world that these explorers were walking into, out there at the 'Ends of the Earth.' While they carried several wonderfully helpful items, the sad reality is that the most prized trading items were sharpened steel weapons and tools. They were a valuable and unknown resource in pre-colonial America. The Franciscans *used those as bribes* for recruiting the native people, sending steel armed allies to kidnap the children of other tribes for converts and slaves.

One of their most famous 'converts' was Chief Solano, who had been stolen from the Suisun tribe, *'the people of the wind,'* to be raised at the Sonoma Mission. He grew into a towering, powerful brave taking for his Christian name the namesake of the mission, Saint Francisco Solano, a Spanish missionary to Peru. The Chief became an important ally and friend of General Vallejo, the military commander of all Spanish, and then later Mexican possessions north of the Bay.

But the native people were not of one mind, and not every tactic worked every time. One tribe that *resolutely resisted the missionaries* and their soldiers was the Napa Wappo, who made their home in the upper valley. This was due to a combination of personality, geology and economics. They were called the 'Wappo', a misnomer from the Spanish word 'guapo' meaning 'handsome and brave,' but the people called themselves the 'Onasatis,' meaning the *'outspoken ones.'* They were a brave people, although their neighbors described them as warlike.

What was it about the Onasatis that made them less susceptible to the Spanish's offers of steel tools, since they could be a wonderful help in the arduous work of providing food and clothing? It's easy to forget that when the Europeans arrived in the Americas the native people *were using stone tools.* The 'Bronze Age' and the 'Iron Age' during which Europe and Asian had developed those technologies had completely bypassed the Americans.

The native people went right from living in the 'Stone Age' to using the technology of the 'Age of Exploration' when steel became widely available. Obviously, sharp tools are important in a hunter-gatherer community, but economically, this *new source of steel tools was competition* for the stone tools that the tribes were using! Where did the stone tools come from? The absolute best came from Napa.

Over the years, the Onasatis had gradually expanded to the south into the Napa Valley from their villages in Northern Sonoma, taking control of an area known today as Glass Mountain. Coincidentally, this is where the 2020 Napa fire began that burned forty percent of the county. In that area there's an abundance of volcanic glass chips that speckle the ground. This black 'obsidian' is the sharpest material on the planet, capable of being sharpened to a single molecule, so even today it's used for the finest scalpels. Not surprisingly it makes sharpest arrowheads, knives, axes and tools. Several local wineries display the tribe's shredding boards.

These long, flat pieces of wood were embedded with hundreds of obsidian chips. They were used by the native people for turning the abundant acorns produced by the stately "valley oaks" into flour, a staple in their diet. The obsidian deposits made the Onasatis *an important part of a trading network* that spread throughout the Bay Area.

The valley's trading trail traveled from the base of Mount Saint Helena in the north, along the eastern hills, above the valley's flood plan, ending in the south at the first wide section of the river near what is today downtown Napa. It *became the basis* for today's Silverado Trail. If you follow the Napa River to the south from there you come to a narrow, watery strait that connects the Sacramento River to the San Pablo Bay, and from there, the San Francisco Bay.

Today that is the site of the Carquinez Bridge. That takes its name for the 'Carquin' tribe that made its home there. In Patwin, the word translates as 'traders,' because they ran the marketplace.

The Onasatis' command of this unique resource made the Spanish and their steel tools competition for this centuries old source of prosperity. The 'Outspoken Ones' ongoing resistance to the invaders ended with them being forcibly removed by the American Cavalry from their *'Talahalusi,' or 'beautiful land,'* to colder settlements on the distant Mendocino Coast. So, the world that the Spanish walked into was a complex culture and trading network they brutally disrupted in their search for gold and converts. But for now, let's leave that sad part of the story behind and get back to the curious story of the wild mustard.

There was another practical reason that the missionaries carried those heavy bags of mustard seeds. Even though the Franciscans had their faults, they were well trained, and it was their job to plot the path that became the Royal Road, *'El Camino Real.* Today the ancient route is marked by a line of shepherd's crooks with bells atop them alongside the highways. The road connected together the sites of California's original twenty-one Franciscan missions.

Following this well-trodden path, you could walk, or ride on horseback, from San Diego to Sonoma in twenty-one days, barring encounters with bears, wolves, rattlesnakes, mountain lions or any native warriors in a bad mood. While the Franciscans depended on the Spanish soldiers for protection, their scholarship and navigation skills made them valuable, albeit demanding leaders.

Today as we drive down our GPS mapped highways, we think of the little mustard seed's contribution to hot dogs and buns, but those Franciscan explorers put the mustard flowers to a clever use. The technique has its origins with the ancient Roman mapmakers, the Roman's loved spicy food and spread their favorite plants, grapes, olives and mustard, throughout their expansive empire!

Like the Romans, the Franciscans carried a bag of mustard seeds with a little hole in the bottom, so it would leave a trail of seeds behind them. In the Spring, when they emerged from their snug Winter quarters and retraced their steps, there would be *lines of the bright yellow flowers springing up*, showing them where they had traveled before. If they needed mustard seeds to spice a meal or compound a remedy, the plants were always handy. It is wonderful to realize that many of California's oldest roads started their lives as paths trimmed with beds of mustard flowers.

Today, the joyful eruption of brightness between the bare vines of Winter is the Franciscan's gift and it's an experience that the locals joyfully anticipate. It also makes our returning wintertime visitors *smile*, because it's a sign that they, like those hearty explorers, have arrived at what the Onasatis called their 'Talahalusi,' their beautiful place.

Chapter Four
Thoroughly Cool Los Carneros

It makes no sense to name a wine region 'Los Carneros,' or 'the Rams,' but that's what the Spanish wrote on the 1820's land-grant that encompassed the rolling hills perched at the southern edge of the Napa and Sonoma Valleys. It's bordered on the south by the San Pablo Bay, an olive-shaped, shallow stretch of water that juts north of the San Francisco Bay. The Spanish couldn't imagine that this cool, windy region would someday produce world class wines. To them, it seemed *a good place to graze their woolly flocks.* Compared to the warmth of the Sonoma Plaza where the Spanish first settled, these hills seemed inhospitable to anyone except shepherds, who are accustomed to a rough life.

Since antiquity, the Ram, or Aries, has been the astrological sign that marks the beginning of Spring. That fits because Los Carneros enjoys a perpetual Spring. Most days are cool, dry, with bright sunshine followed by cold nights. The North Bay is *a place of extremes* and Los Carneros is at the forefront of that. One of the secrets of the North Bay's talent for growing wine grapes is the glassy surface of the San Pablo Bay. It acts as a mirror, casting the reflected sunshine to the north creating what The Weather Channel calls 'abundant sunshine'. The vineyards that sit closest to that mirror are in Los Carneros.

But the strength of the sunlight is not the only factor. At night, the cool fog rolls in from the bay, blanketing Los Carneros before traveling up the valleys like a misty river. In the morning, it withdraws south and eventually slips out through the Golden Gate, like a Genie returning to their bottle. That leaves the local vineyards shrouded in fog much longer than the northern valleys. As the morning sunshine grows stronger it travels through a refractive filter of water particles, creating *color-filled rainbows* that the wine grapes turn into micro-nutrients that we experience as flavors!

This is important wherever the fog travels, but it is most at home in Los Carneros and coincidentally, where they grow the same grape varietals as in the Russian River Valley, Chardonnay and Pinot Noir. This band of land along the bay is geologically different from the warmer valleys to the north. Under its rolling green hills lies an *ancient, basaltic seabed* which adds crispness to the wines. That's different from the volcanic ridges and iron rich riverbeds found in the upper valleys that promote great depth of flavors in the wines. The brightness encouraged by the basalt rich soil is one of the reasons that the sparkling wines have done so well here.

Then there's the wind! Every day, the Los Carneros wind comes in off the San Pablo Bay and soars over the hills like a great nature spirit. Grapevines are sensitive to wind and when it blows too strongly, the leaves close their pores to preserve their moisture and the vine stops making sugar. This short circuit in the growing cycle allows the thin-skinned grapes, like Pinot Noir, enough time to make the deeper flavors that people prize, without producing the excessive sugar that would turn into ballistic alcohol in the finished wine. While high alcohol sounds like fun, it's not graceful, the careful balancing of diverse components is at the heart of great winemaking.

Los Carneros is obviously unique in the region but how and when did it become a premium vineyard site? These days, when Napa and Sonoma wines are famous for their quality, it's easy to forget that for much of their history they grew inexpensive grapes. Truly little of their fruit was made into wine inside the counties.

Instead, starting in the 1800's, they were shipped to wineries closer to the city, and there was rarely a mention of a grape variety or location, the wines were red or white, sweet or hearty. Thanks to a number of cultural, economic and governmental reasons, the shift in the region from jug wines to premiums started in the 1970's. Then it really took off after the turn of the millennium.

While the location of a winery is flexible, the location of the vineyards is not.

From the cool southern edges of the bay to the warm tops of the valleys, the climate changes dramatically. This is due to the influence of the bay, the ocean and the rocky hills bordering the northern valleys, which are perfect for capturing the sun's heat. Napa is warmer than Sonoma because it's farther from the cool Pacific. Also, Napa Valley has Mount Saint Helena towering over its northern edge, *protecting it from the* north *winds*. Farming is all about location, so the growers carefully choose the best vineyard sites for the types of wine they want to make.

Traditionally, the growing areas like the Sonoma Valley and Napa's Oakville were always more popular because the warmth helps the grapes ripen sooner. In a competitive, bulk market, growers want their grapes to be ready to harvest as early as possible. *Only a certain number of grapes are going to be sold every year* and the sooner you can get to market the better chance you have of selling every bunch for the best price.

Also, the sooner you brought in the fruit, the less chance your crop would be damaged by any early rains. In the past when there were plenty of vineyard sites to go around, that left cooler Los Carneros and nearby Coombsville as suitable places to raise cattle, sheep and horses.

The rise of Los Carneros as a place to grow premium grapes is an interesting and complicated story. In the early days up-valley growers planted Riesling,

Pinot Noir and Chardonnay next to the Cabernet, Merlot and Zinfandel. But the regions where those diverse varieties thrive in Europe are hundreds and sometimes thousands of miles apart, with quite different climates. To understand why growers would move vineyards to a cooler climate we need to understand how vines work. The bright flavors that we so enjoy in wines are made in the grapes from sunlight and the deep flavors are contributed by the wood.

When Galileo said, *"Wine is water held together by sunshine,"* in many ways, he was correct. Imagine the sun rising in the vineyard, the earth warming and the sap creeping up the vine towards the grapes. As the sap moves through those twists and turns, it creates the aromatic textures that give the wine its foundation. That's why an older, kinkier vine produces more flavor than a young one with its smooth trunk. Vines need about one hundred days of the sap rising and falling to make enough of these complex, textured flavors to create an exceptional wine.

The red Burgundy grape Pinot Noir, thanks to its thin skin, will quickly produce enough alcohol for an entertaining wine. But, that hot, daylong sunshine found in the upper valleys helps the grapes produce sugar so quickly that the vine's sap doesn't have enough days to create those deeper flavors that give it character.

That's like a great looking person with *lots of sex appeal, but not a thought in their head!* They're attractive short-term, but iffy for a committed relationship. Who helped the local growers figure out where to plant their delicate, refined Pinot Noir vines, and their favorite companion grape, Chardonnay?

In the 1970s the godfather of winemaking in the North Bay was a diminutive Russian émigré named André Tchelistcheff. He came from a wealthy Russian family that had left the service of the Tzar during the revolution. After being *left for dead on the battlefield* in the conflict between the Red and White Russian armies, André arrived in Paris. There he studied winemaking, eventually arriving at the Pasteur Institute in Paris, which was the Mecca of the still new fermentation sciences.

Georges de La Tour, a Frenchman and chemist who was the head of Beaulieu Vineyards in Napa, found André there and invited him to be his winemaker. Since André had the required adventurous blood, he came to California and took the reins at Beaulieu and later Buena Vista. Thanks to his personal genius and the lack of restraints found in a new world winery, he proved to be an amazing innovator in wine technology.

Besides his career crafting some of America's early great wines, he was also the most important vineyard consultant in the region, responsible for planning numerous important winery properties. You can bet that if André once laid out the plans for their original vineyards, that factoid is going to appear on a winery's website. When you visit Beaulieu, there's a life-sized statue of André in the garden outside the reserve room.

In a funny twist of *hero worship*, when the Culinary Institute of America bought the Copia Center for Wine, Food and the Arts in downtown Napa, they commissioned a copy of the statue, but they enlarged it. They felt that a 'true to size' sculpture of the 4' 11" André was not impressive enough for the entranceway, so he got pumped up!

In the 1970s when the pace of grape growing accelerated and investments started flowing into the North Bay wineries, André, with Pinot Noir and Chardonnay cuttings in hand, led the charge to Los Carneros. He explained to everyone who would listen that it was *too hot up valley for these cool weather vines.* If they would plant the vines in the cooler climate that they preferred, they would make better wines. He was right!

It was around that time when promoters started calling Los Carneros the *'Burgundy of America,'* after France's primary Pinot producing region. It's the only AVA, or American Viticultural Area, which is shared by Napa and Sonoma. That's probably because it was established in the early 1980s before Napa was such a prominent brand.

They wouldn't share an AVA today because Napa *does not play well with others* and it's very protective of its brand name. Although, with Los Carneros, there's good justification for including the entire area as one district. Along the entire length it has a similar climate and geology, and a limited number of premium grape varieties grow well there.

Trying to grow warmer weather grapes like Cabernet or Merlot in Los Carneros often produces green pepper flavors that appear when the grapes struggle to ripen completely. From my own narrow perspective,

I wonder if the Sonoma Coast is a better example of the American Burgundy, with their great forests and ocean influence. The Pinot Noir from there shows that classic earthy depth of flavor more easily. In contrast, based on the spectacular Vermentino wines, an Italian white variety that I've had from Los Carneros, I wonder if calling it the 'American Cinque Terra' would be more accurate?

When the lines for the AVA were drawn, Napa made their part of Los Carneros larger than Sonoma's by generously extending it *up into the rolling hills* at the foot of Mount Veeder. In Sonoma they were more conservative with their pen. The Sonoma side of Los Carneros tightly hugs the bay and stops at the road that connects the two counties called predictably, Carneros Highway.

Just north of the road, the vineyards are considered to be in the Sonoma Valley AVA, even though that area south of the Sonoma Plaza grows the same grape varieties as Los Carneros. They felt that the Sonoma Valley AVA, which had been created a few years before, was a stronger brand than Los Carneros, but they didn't want to let Napa claim the AVA all for itself. *This tradition of drawing lines for the maximum financial advantage has a long tradition in California.*

In 1850 when it was about to become a state, California insisted on drawing its own borders. That's why the northeast border is on the far side of the gold-bearing mountains, to the detriment of Nevada. At the southern border, the line cants to the southwest to place the spectacular San Diego Harbor inside the United States, over the objections of Mexico.

I don't know if André had counted fully on the advantages that come from those dependable Carneros winds. Not only do they reduce the alcohol levels, but they help the grapes retain the valuable acids that clean the palate between bites, making the food taste better. It also helps your digestion by supplementing the stomach acid, which gets weaker as we get older. While a low acid wine like white Zinfandel is so soft on the palate that it makes a great cocktail drink, it doesn't make a meal taste better.

But a high-acid, Los Carneros wine excels at that. Also, the three acids in grapes contribute to the flavor and appeal, with tartaric being the savory acid most associated with wine. The citric acid that is common in oranges and lemons, and the malic acid that is found in apples contribute their own grace notes, although winemakers will often work to tone down the malic acid.

When wine is aged in oak barrels, a significant amount of that *malic acid is converted into lactic acid,* also found in fermented dairy. In red wines that softens the wine but in white wines it can also create the buttery flavor found in some popular chardonnays.

When grapes are grown in a location where it stays hot at night, the vines dump the acids, so the winemakers add tartaric acid because it's an essential part of wine's signature flavor! But those wines lack dimension, although they have plenty of alcohol. That's why those cold Los Carneros nights, which make the vines shiver, make all the difference when the wine gets to the glass. To give you an idea of how much winemakers value the acids in a grape, when the final product lacks that important structural feature they call it a 'flabby wine.' There's no situation when 'flabby' can pass as a compliment and you would never describe the cool climate Los Carneros wines that way!

Starting in the 1970s, as news of the area's potential spread, the European winemakers took notice. When they heard Chardonnay and Pinot Noir they thought Champagne, because those are the preferred grapes used in their famous sparkling wines. *As a result,* when you are standing at the foot of the Napa Valley on the patio at Domaine Carneros, owned by the Taittinger family from Champagne, France, European winemakers surround you. Across the road to the south, Cuvaison Estate Wines is owned by the Schmidheiny family from Switzerland. 'Cuvaison' in French is the process of extracting the colors and flavors from the skins of the grapes.

To the north, across the Carneros Highway and just beyond the di Rosa sculpture park, is the Artesa Winery, owned by Spain's oldest winemaking family, Raventós Codorníu. The name Artesa means *'craftsman'* in Catalan, the language in the region around Barcelona where the family is from. The modern, minimalistic building is tucked between two hills and built into the top of a third. They began by making sparkling wines in Napa in the early 1980's but ran into two roadblocks.

First, Americans *don't drink as much sparkling wine* as Europeans. Second, they were in direct competition with Domaine Carneros, that also makes sparkling wines. But Domaine is more visible and conveniently located in a grand Chateau that looks like a brick wedding cake, dramatically towering over the road. In comparison, Artesa is tucked in the hills, down a small road, in an earth covered building. It's a remarkable experience once you get inside, but you need to know that it's there! This must have been *very embarrassing* for the Codorníu family who have been making wine since the 1500s. How do they explain to the rest of the family that their winery in Napa is in the red? But, once they recognized the issues they shifted their focus to still wines, which Americans drink in abundance, and sales improved dramatically.

Just to the west of Artesa are the Carneros vineyards of Mumm (The French pronunciation is like moon, but with the M at the end /m/u:/m/ Moom), another French company from Champagne. They very smartly did not place their winery here. Instead, their winery and tasting room are halfway up the Napa Valley on the Silverado Trail in Rutherford. Because they are the only sparkling wine producer in the neighborhood, they have the dual advantage of being unique and convenient.

Further to the west, over the county line in Sonoma's Los Carneros, Gloria Ferrer from Spain produces marvelous sparkling wines on their large estate. They are *one of the first wineries you see* when you come north from San Francisco and their vineyards are spread out alongside the road at the foot of the hills. They chose that land because it reminded them of the area around their Catalan vineyards, so they built a rambling Spanish style winery. They dug caves for aging under the winery and built an exceedingly popular and expansive patio that looks over their vineyards to the northern edges of the bay. Obviously, the Europeans love Los Carneros and the fact that it's such a short drive from San Francisco ensures them plenty of visitors.

After an absence of many years, the herds of *grazing sheep have returned to Los Carneros*. Once the winter rains have filled the rows between the bare vines with tall grass and yellow mustard, you can see their fluffy white coats between the vines. Their gradual grazing works better than any plow at restoring the health of the land.

As they consume the springtime greens, they fertilize the land, while their hooves stomp on the bugs, promoting the secret life of the soil where flavor begins in magical ways. We are seeing them among the vines throughout the region, in part because a vineyard tended by sheep rather than rototillers eventually needs half as much water.

That quality is incredibly valuable in perpetually parched California. Whenever we see a flock of 'los carneros' grazing between the vines, we look for their *guardian dogs nearby,* keeping an eye open for coyotes and mountain lions, and looking right at home.

For all the large wineries in Los Carneros, there are still plenty of family ranches producing much smaller volumes of high-quality wine. Between the vineyards of Artesa and Mumm are the Fulton Vineyards, whose line of flagpoles, perched on a rise, can be seen from the Carneros Highway. It can be hard for a grape grower, living on their own land, dealing with the ramifications of decisions made in distant corporate boardrooms on the other side of the ocean.

Clearly, as a statement of their independence, the Hudson family runs the '*Jolly Roger*' pirate flag up their western-most flagpole twice a year. This is done to celebrate bud-break in the Spring when the vines first show their new leaves, and at harvest time, when the grapes are coming into the winery. This is a bay area custom that is popular among family businesses when they are surrounded by corporate entities. Flying the 'Jolly Roger' also brings a *smile* to those passing by.

Above: General Mariano Guadalupe Vallejo
Opposite: Sonoma Mission

Chapter Five
They All Came to Sonoma

One of California's most historic and charming locations, the Sonoma Plaza, is only half an hour's drive north of the Golden Gate. It's a spacious, tree-covered park with Mediterranean roots, which provides a central square for a town hall, stores, restaurants and cafes for the locals to meet. The only thing the Plaza lacks is an 'active church' although the historic Sonoma Mission's chapel on the northeast corner once filled that role. Surprisingly for such a tiny town, it's California's largest Plaza, so it easily accommodates the symmetrical city hall at its center.

The building was constructed with four identical sides to please the tax paying shopkeepers, because none of them wanted their stores to face the back of the building. Sonoma's special place in California history starts with being the northernmost, and final official outpost of the Spanish Empire in the Americas, and the final Franciscan Mission. I like to think that the explorers got this far and said, "Clearly we've arrived in Eden, this is far enough."

In front of the Sonoma Mission is a metal shepherd's crook with a bell at its top. These markers appear along the southern half of California on the historic path of El Camino Real. This "Royal Road" connected Spanish settlements together in North America.

In California most notably, it traveled between the twenty-one missions from San Diego to Sonoma where the Royal Road ended. Despite its grand title, in many places it would have been a narrow, horse trodden pathway, fringed with yellow mustard flowers.

The Plaza was laid out in 1835 by General Mariano Guadalupe Vallejo, a native born "Californio", who was the Spanish, and then Mexican commandant of Northern California. He hired a British sailor to help him survey the streets of the town. The old salt had good navigation skills because they aligned the streets quite accurately with the true compass directions.

The arrangement of the Plaza is *a bit unconventional.* Like most plazas it connects to four roads at the corners. But the Sonoma Plaza also had to accommodate El Camino Real, which connected to the center of the Plaza at the southern edge. Today it is called Broadway and when you drive up it towards the Plaza you are pointed due north! That same 'broad way' also once connected the Plaza to the docks twelve miles south on the San Pablo Bay. There the road heads west before turning south and following the edge of the bay to the Mission town of San Rafael.

The dramatic result of this design is that today, when visitors approach downtown Sonoma, they drive up a wide road lined with trees shading attractive homes, and arrive at the center of the Plaza, with the picturesque city hall directly in front of them.

The terrain between the Plaza and the bay is level, fertile farmland. So, when the General built a tower at the north edge of the Plaza, beside the barracks, any soldier on watch could see for many miles to the south. To the north, the land rapidly rises into a ridge of heavily forested hills that protect the town from the winter winds coming down the valley. *This was a wise choice for the town's location, and it was entirely thanks to General Vallejo.*

In contrast, the Franciscans had originally established the Mission in a less than ideal location six miles south, closer to the bay where it was subject to the relentless 'Carneros wind' and the nightly fogs!

Today the Cline Family Winery sits on that site. The family constructed a Mission Museum on their property, featuring models of the twenty-one missions built by German craftsmen for The Golden Gate International Exposition in 1939. The models had been in storage for many years when they were put up for auction and the Cline's purchased the entire lot, and then had them restored.

Northern California at that time was considered the 'ends of the earth,' where you sent your 'red headed stepchild' to make their fortune. If they did good, that's great, and if they didn't, well, who would know? Yet, the adventurous at heart from around the world kept finding their way there and as a result, seven different national flags have flown over Sonoma. You can see them in front of the city hall and around the corner at the Sebastiani Winery, next to the area's oldest vineyard site.

The flags start with England, when Sir Francis Drake planted his colors at Bodega Bay, during his circumnavigation of the globe in the 1600's in his ship, the Golden Hind. Then in 1820 Sonoma saw the flag of Imperial Spain raised with the establishment of the Presidio, or Fort, after which the Mission was relocated there.

Then the Spanish flag was replaced with that of Imperial Mexico under the Emperor Maximillian, a nephew of Napoleon. Next, power was wrested away from Maximillian in the Mexican Revolution, most flamboyantly by Pancho Villa. When the flag of the Republic of Mexico was raised the new government, in faraway Mexico City, secularized the missions, considering them, justifiably, as an instrument of the monarchy.

Someplace in this mix the flag of Imperial Russia flew at their Fort Ross, or 'Rossiya,' (Ruh-syee-yuh) for 'Mother Russia.' They established their 'fort' on the Northern Sonoma coast to grow food for their settlements in Alaska, under the noses of the Spanish and English, who had previous claims nearby. They also launched expeditions of Kodiak hunters from

Alaska along the California coast aboard American sailing ships, to hunt the sea otters for their precious pelts.

On June 14th, 1846, coincidentally America's 'Flag Day', American revolutionaries, mostly from Napa, raised the Bear Flag of the California Republic on the Plaza, in front of the barracks. Soon after, the first American naval ship of the line sailed into the San Francisco Bay, and the next flag to fly over Sonoma was the American. Sonoma became the United States military headquarters for Northern California and was frequented by numerous Civil War generals. *The old officer's quarters are still there* on Spain Street, walking distance from the Plaza, is the home of the commandant, Colonel Hooker, a Civil War hero. So, even though it was far from everywhere important at that time, plenty of countries wanted to stake a claim to Sonoma.

In the 1800's Sonoma was a mix of the native tribes, colonial Spanish, adventurous Americans, hospitable Russians and finally the industrious Chinese. The first Chinese ship sailed through the Golden Gate in 1850. In drawings and paintings of the wineries from that era, large numbers of Chinese workers are seen carrying and crushing grapes.

The oldest wine caves were dug by Chinese workers, who also cleared vineyards and built the bordering stone walls. From a Eurocentric point of view, it's important to realize that even though the Spanish left a cultural mark on colonial Sonoma, it sits on the Pacific Rim, where the Asian influence is ancient and pervasive. The one flag that has not been acknowledged is that of the

Chinese Admiral Zheng He, whose ships came to the California coast in the 1400s, as one of his seven Treasure fleets that sailed the globe and created the first known world maps.

The West Coast is littered with *artifacts left behind by the great treasure fleet;* stone anchors, buried shipwrecks and armor. The early Spanish cartographers frequently postulated locations for a Chinese city on the Northern California coast, that they named Quivira. That is also the name of a Northern Sonoma winery in the Dry Creek Valley, where the founder once displayed their collection of those historic maps in a small gallery beside the tasting room. Unfortunately, when they sold the winery, the maps left with them.

In the late 1800s, thirty percent of the Sonoma Plaza was filled with Chinese shops. At that time the important destination was a pair of towns several miles north of the Plaza thanks to numerous healing hot springs, around which hotels had sprung up to serve guests coming from the city.

After the 1906 earthquake that devastated San Francisco, the springs mysteriously receded into the earth and the businesses dried up. Today, only the Sonoma Mission Inn remains, and it accesses the deep mineral springs with a well. The rest of those investors moved south to the Plaza, forcing the Chinese businesses out.

In so many ways a plaza is different from a park, because it's a central meeting place for the community. Similar layouts are found in plazas throughout southern Europe and Northern Africa, remnants of the Roman

Empire which once ruled that part of the world. When Roman armies made camp, they used a similar layout, with a large open space for the troops to assemble, directly to the south of the commander's tent, or their house if it was a winter camp. General Vallejo, a classically trained soldier, mimicked that arrangement, and placed his initial home and headquarters on the northern edge of the Plaza, where he drilled his troops.

Despite the many purposes the Plaza has been used for over the years, today it is a beautiful location, thanks to the Women's Club of Sonoma. In the early 1900's the Plaza was a wreck, with numerous holes where mud for the adobe buildings had been excavated, and the debris from its short use as a railway terminal. The local club took the initiative and began a landscaping and tree planting campaign which yielded wonderful results.

Today there are two playgrounds, picnic tables, a duck pond, a band shell, a Visitors Center in an old Carnegie library, and plenty of space for multiple outdoor events like art and car shows. It is all wonderfully shaded by a spectacular and diverse grove of trees. There is also a charming statue of a seated General Vallejo, who would be pleased to see how the Plaza has evolved.

At the time when the Spanish established a Mission and Fort in San Francisco their resources were stretched *ridiculously thin*. They had colonies in south, Central and North America and bases in the far-off Philippines. The Missions depended on enslaving the local tribes people to operate, but there were very few trained soldiers available to enforce that. It was improbable that the Spanish could maintain control over California with the feisty Americans so nearby, by both sea and land.

Considering the potential of the San Francisco Bay, the Spanish Governor couldn't resist putting a Fort and Mission there. Unfortunately, the San Francisco Dolores Mission, was well named, because 'Dolores' translates as 'Sorrows' and it was not a happy place; cold, foggy, plagued with malaria and hard to supply.

Admittedly the monks did choose *the warmest spot in that very cool peninsula for the mission,* and the park nearby is the spot where modern San Franciscans go when they are craving some sunshine. Despite that the monks and native helpers often sickened, so forty difficult years later they established a sanatorium eleven miles north of the Golden Gate at the warmer and dryer Mission at Saint Rafael. So now they had two missions, that due to climate and distance, were about as effective as two drunks helping each other walk down the street.

Up to this time two highly capable Franciscan Fathers, Junipero Serra and Fermín de Lasuén, had been directing the establishment of these settlements from the lovely Mission at Carmel. By the time San Rafael was established the Spanish grip on California was getting increasingly wobbly. Even though it's only one hundred and twenty miles from Carmel to San Francisco, due to the dangerous fog bound entrance to the bay, the marshes, and some very unfriendly tribes, it was a hard trip by land and sea. That made the two northernmost missions of San Francisco and San Rafael less than prime posts.

When a brash young Franciscan from Barcelona named Jose Altimira arrived in Carmel, Lasuén sent this unpleasant youngster to Mission Dolores, likely thinking, *"How much damage could he do?"*

Meanwhile to the north, the Russians had established their Fort Ross on the Sonoma Coast and were starting to trade further south. In this geopolitical game of chess, the Spanish commander wanted to establish a foothold in the North Bay to curtail that expansion. Since the Franciscan Missionaries worked hand in hand with the military, the young firebrand monk, Altimira, eventually proposed closing the missions in cool, wet San Francisco and nearby San Rafael, and using those resources to establish a mission farther north in Sonoma.

The commander gave him permission, and a few soldiers, to scout for a new site. This was a breach of protocol since he should have contacted the church fathers for permission, who, knowing Altimira, would have said no! But they set out to find a spot for the new spiritual outpost.

Of experience and judgment, Altimira was sorely lacking, because he chose a site in the first line of rolling hills above the bay. The location was cool, foggy, and perilously close to the malarial swamps that once lined the bay. It was barely an improvement on Yerba Buena, as San Francisco was known. At least on the bay they were close to the docks that brought their supplies. He called it the 'Mission San Francisco,' so now there were two of them. Why didn't he establish the settlement ten miles north in the warm, dry Sonoma Valley, a virtual paradise for growing food? Because they encountered native tribes that were not very welcoming to these interlopers. Even though he established the new mission, the Franciscans never closed the one in the south, so to differentiate between them they added the name Solano to the Sonoma Mission, for a south American missionary who had been made a Saint.

Altamira was remarkably bad at endearing himself to the native people, whom they depended upon for converts and labor. To save him from harm the Franciscan Fathers in Carmel quickly transferred him to another mission. Soon after the government in Mexico decreed that all Spanish born people, unwilling to become Mexican citizens, must leave Alta California and he returned to Spain, never to be heard from again, although his name graces a Sonoma Middle School.

A while later, now 'General' Vallejo, who had a keen eye for real estate, moved the mission to the warmth and safety of the Sonoma Plaza, where it sits today as a state museum. So that is how downtown Sonoma ended up in the only nearby valley without a river.

Today the population of the little City of Sonoma is just over 10,000 people. Considering the expansiveness of the Plaza, I suspect that the General expected it to grow much larger with time. But despite being at the base of a wonderfully fertile valley, as an economic center, it suffered from a serious flaw. There is no river or docks, and without those there would be no boats nearby to economically carry the farm produce to market. Most major cities are on navigable rivers. The exceptions are places like Denver, which is a stopping off point before crossing the mountains. Even though Rome's Tiber River only handles small boats, it became a commercial center because travelers on the ancient salt trail could safely ford the river there.

The Spanish choice of Sonoma as a Pueblo, or official city, and a military base seems odd, because just to the west is the city of Petaluma, which sits on the northern edge of the navigable Petaluma River. About the same distance to the east is the city of Napa, on the banks of the navigable Napa River. Maybe General Vallejo thought Petaluma too cold and Napa too hot, so Sonoma in the middle was just right, and at the center of the territory he firmly controlled.

There was one *unexpected benefit that came from Sonoma being an economic backwater,* compared to its neighboring cities with their navigable rivers; it remained small and frugal. So, rather than replacing older buildings with newer construction, including the original and very charming adobes, they could only afford to repair what they had.

As a result, downtown Sonoma has a wonderful collection of buildings from the founding period of California. In comparison, larger and wealthier Napa and Petaluma have an impressive collection of European style stone buildings that were constructed later in the 1800's and early 1900's, when lumber and wine shipping created a steady stream of wealth.

As roads and cars improved, the quaint nature of Sonoma, with its history, wine and charming Plaza, became wonderfully attractive to tourists wanting to spend a day in the country. The tiny town of Sonoma is the most historic spot in California, a commonwealth that, in land mass, is similar to Japan or Italy.

Here's why! Sonoma was home to California's 21st and final Franciscan mission. It was also the sixth and final official Spanish city, or 'Pueblo'. Then it was one of a handful of official forts, or Presidios. It is the only town in California that has all three of these historical distinctions. Finally, it's the 'Philadelphia of California,' because the Sonoma Plaza was where California declared itself the Independent Republic of California. They raised the 'Bear Flag' there on the northeastern corner of the Plaza in front of the Mexican soldier's barracks, which are still there today as part of the state park.

You can recognize the site by the statue celebrating the 'Bear Flaggers.' Their choice of the 'Bear' flag, which is today the state flag, is due to an interesting piece of history. At the time the settlers arrived, the North Bay had one of the largest populations of California grizzly bears on the West Coast. To stay safe the early settlers were forced to make their homes up in the trees, and for tribes outside the region the word 'Napa' meant grizzly bear.

While all this sounds quite heroic, there's some shading that we need to add to the story. The Bear Flaggers who bearded General Vallejo in his den included about thirty Americans, mostly from Napa. They had heard rumors that the Mexican government was going to force them out. While this was proposed by the Governor in Monterey, it was not very likely. First of all, there were lots of Americans in the area, mostly arriving by ship, although some came over the mountains via the Donner Pass. Second, General Vallejo liked the Americans, he gave many of them land for services rendered, and he was having a hard enough time finding Mexicans and Native People to develop the wonderful farm and grazing land.

So, he wasn't inclined to force out any good prospects. He told people that his birthday was on July fourth, Independence Day, even though it was actually on the fifth, because he felt that California's future was with the United States. Also, he depended on the American sailing ships to bring him needed goods.

In fact, his house was brought from *New England* in pieces in the belly of *an American sailing ship.* Later he bought a second house, transported the same way, that he gave to his daughter. Both houses stand today, one on a local park made from the Vallejo Farmstead, and the other as a restaurant on Spain Street called predictably, 'The General's Daughter.'

Was it good luck or planning, that the revolutionaries arrived at the barracks when the General's soldiers were away on missions? General Vallejo was there by himself, with an armed company of former soldiers on his front steps. So, he invited the leaders in to talk and broke out the brandy, of which he was one of the North Bay's biggest producers.

The discussion was long-winded, because after the leaders had not emerged for several hours, they sent another representative inside, who found the little group having a wonderful time. But rather than returning to make a report to the waiting band, they also joined in the festivities. Eventually the General invited everyone to his place for dinner and the first day of the revolution came to an inebriated close.

That custom of the Plaza being a place for hospitality, and the coming together of people to find a common ground is a long tradition that continues there today.

The final Shepherd's Crook and Bell at the Sonoma
Mission Marking the Route of the Camino Royale

Chapter Six
The Magical Valley of the Moon

As you travel north from San Francisco through the hills of Marin County, when you turn east at the top of the bay you quickly enter the lower edges of Sonoma County. As you go over a low hill called Sears Point, that can be seen from miles away on the bay, you are in the Los Carneros region, known for its windy, cool climate and extensive chardonnay and pinot noir vineyards. As you travel north you enter the lovely Sonoma Valley. The rocky Mayacamas Mountains form the valley's eastern side while the graceful Petaluma Hills and Sonoma Mountain form the western edge. Twelve miles north of the bay you come to the little, charming town of Sonoma.

The origin of the name Sonoma has invited many opinions. In the native Patwin or Pomo languages Sonoma means the Valley of the Moon. So, the name, Sonoma Valley, means 'Valley of the Moon' Valley! Odd, but in California there are many examples of names made up of merged languages. *The North Bay has more native names than much of California* because the local tribes were prosperous, the grizzly bears were fierce, and the three competing groups of colonizers were stretched thin as they vied for control. Sonoma is a popular name used in numerous brands, Williams Sonoma being the most famous, having started his store steps from the Plaza.

Locally it seems like every other organization and business is called 'Sonoma' something or other, including the County of Sonoma, the City of Sonoma, the Sonoma Plaza, the Sonoma Valley, Sonoma Mountain, the Sonoma Women's Club and half of the businesses.

Surprisingly, there's no Sonoma River and that is a place where the historic city was short-changed, because Napa to the east and Petaluma to the west both have navigable rivers, not surprisingly named for them. From their downtown docks you can sail to the bay, the Pacific Ocean and the world beyond.

But Sonoma Valley is drained by a humble, but pretty stream called predictably, Sonoma Creek. The northern part of the county is drained by the long, but shallow Russian River, which empties into the Pacific north of Bodega Bay. But the only craft traveling along that waterway, as it wends its way through vineyards and forests are canoes, rafts and inner tubes filled with vacationers.

The complete story of the name 'Sonoma' is complicated by the remarkable history of the North Bay, which I've been told is the longest continuously occupied region in North America. For people who understand agriculture that fact is not surprising, because the geology and climate are especially favorable for humans and the plants that feed them. A good part of California has the prized Mediterranean climate, and the North Bay is the center of that zone. It's a place of warm, dry days with brilliant sunshine, and cool, humid nights.

We owe credit for the translation of the name Sonoma to a giant of the literary world, Jack London. He was a hard living, hard drinking, cigarette smoking adventurer. As a teenager he'd been an 'oyster pirate' on the San Francisco Bay, in a boat that he bought with money borrowed from the part-African American, part-Caucasian woman who raised him. When he returned from prospecting in Alaska with empty pockets, he became America's most successful author by writing about his time there.

Later, Jack taught himself how to navigate by the stars while sailing to Hawaii. As money rolled in, he bought a thousand acres on the slopes of Sonoma Mountain, above the tiny town of Glen Ellen, that he called his "Beauty Ranch." He practiced an early version of sustainable agriculture and railed at his neighbors for their less environmentally friendly practices. While he grew wine grapes on vineyards that are still there, he didn't make wine. So, he would ride his horse down the hill to his neighbors who were very proper, church-going folks, whose busy farm included a sawmill, vineyards and most importantly, a winery. He would hitch his horse to a rail outside their office and purchase some bottles. The Missus disliked the colorful Mr. London's lifestyle and the moment he was late in his accounts, she would cut him off.

Some of her resentment may have come from the strained arrangement of their property lines, often an issue in farming communities, because Jack's ranch surrounded their lovely little valley. Their land had been a grant from General Vallejo, in thanks for carpentry work that the husband had done repairing Sonoma's Mission building. Today that ranch is the site of the Benziger Family Winery, with its elegant, terraced vineyards. The original farm buildings where Jack used to hitch his horse on his wine runs are still there, although under occasional attack by some particularly aggressive woodpeckers.

At the time when Jack London settled in Sonoma, there were several native tribes in the area that had been converted to Christianity by the Franciscan Missionaries and allied themselves with General Vallejo. Most notable among them was Sem-Yeto, who everybody called Chief Solano. At six foot, seven inches tall he was an impressively powerful man. He took his name from the San Francisco Solano Mission in Sonoma where he was educated, after being kidnapped as a child from the Suisun tribe over the mountains to the east.

Sem-Yeto was a close friend of the General and quite a famous personality in the region and seen as the titular head of all the Sonoma tribes. *The Chief took quite a fancy to the Russian Princess Helene de Gagarin,* the wife of General (or Count depending on the telling) Alexander Rotscheff from Fort Ross. Sem-Yeto made plans to kidnap her with the help of the other chiefs. But Vallejo talked him out of that, by describing how the combined forces of the Spanish and the Russians would set out to annihilate the tribes. So, for the sake of his people he sacrificed his desire for the blonde beauty.

It's funny that the two Missions named for Saint Francis are at the far northern edge of his order's circle of influence in the Americas. Supposedly, as Friar Junipero Serra sailed up the California coast naming bays for every saint except their patron, he told the soldiers that Francis would let him know when they had come to his place.

Since the San Francisco Bay is among the world's greatest, it seemed a natural fit. It was only through a later misguided effort to move the Mission to Sonoma, that they ended up with two missions named for Francis, which the Franciscans seemed fine with. What's interesting is that the Sonoma Mission, which takes its primary name from the native language, is the only one that has a memorial to the many native people who lived and served there.

When Jack London settled into his new home in the early 1900's there was still a large population of native people in the area. It's not surprising that Jack London, who made his living as a writer, asked around about the meaning of Sonoma. A local Chief told him that Sonoma meant the *Valley of the Seven Moons.* That makes sense since the Patwin word for Moon is 'Sanar,' from which Sonoma is a short trip, especially if the word for place, or home is 'Ma.' That is coincidentally one of the first 'words' that babies make, hence: mom, mama, madre, mother. Also, the Sonoma Valley where Jack lived is crescent, or Moon shaped so it all fits.

When trying to understand why they would say seven moons we need to realize that, unlike today, the native people would have had a more personal relationship with the sky. The Sun ruled their days, and the Moon their nights. Nighttime travel was timed to the lunations. Venus was the most beautiful jewel in their sky while Mars looked blood red. Mercury shone brightly for the briefest moments like the arrival of a brilliant idea. Jupiter and Saturn's orbits marked the longer cycles of life. Maybe seven Moons was a mistranslation for the Pomo word for *the seven celestial bodies,* the Sun, Moon and Planets, that all of humanity has watched travel through the heavens during countless millennia.

But they were not the only pre-Columbian residents of Sonoma with sky knowledge. We know that Chinese sailors were left behind by the Treasure fleets in the 1400's. Besides the stone anchors and armor later discovered, the Bay Area also has a very long wall in the east bay. It was built with the same construction techniques used in China's Great Wall, and its origin has never been explained. The Spanish encountered tribes in Northern California that wore Chinese style clothes and hair styles. In the late 1800's a state anthropologist found a tribe of 'Indians' living in the Russian River Valley's redwood forests *that only spoke Chinese.*

Sailors, more than most people, are tied to the stars. Traveling the open seas, devoid of distracting light under the dome of the heavens, they depend on the seven celestial bodies that travel the ecliptic for guidance. The Chinese were among the ancient world's most advanced astronomers and cartographers, and their *Astrologers* considered the planets reflections of the social hierarchy on Earth. The Sun was the Emperor, the Moon the Empress, Mercury their secretary, messenger and servant, Venus represented the court ladies, while Mars represented the court guards, Jupiter stood for the educated Mandarins and Saturn stood for the Priests.

They observed the planets as they changed positions, and angled for power, meeting, separating, and shaping the fates of those below. *The Chinese Compass,* or Bagua, is used for both *navigation and Feng Shui.* It divides the world into eight directions, seven for the celestial bodies, and one for the Earth beneath our feet. How much of the Chinese sailor's knowledge seeped into the lore of the native tribes?

Compared to sunnier, warmer Napa, Sonoma has always been considered mysterious. It is divided into numerous unique valleys, towering redwood forests and convoluted coastlines. The climate and geology vary widely, but among all these diverse locations Sonoma Valley is special. It was formed in a gentle crescent between two lines of mountains, the remains of ancient volcanoes and uplifted seabed, that are steep, but not inaccessible. It is only fifteen miles long and varies between one and two miles wide. At its northern edge is the broad Santa Rosa plain. To the south are gently rolling hills that turn into the marshes of the San Pablo Bay.

The little City of Sonoma sits like a pearl in the lower third of its elongated crescent. The valley sits in a magic zone, where everything grows well. There are numerous underground springs that not only provide the plants with water, but also minerals. The soil is especially good at *holding onto that water,* and because the valley is narrow it loses less moisture to the hot sun. The valley angles from the northwest to the southeast, perfectly aligned with the warm, color rich mid-morning sunshine.

So, what is the source of the name Sonoma? There are so many possibilities. Who knows what the Chief was trying to explain when he 'translated' the name Sonoma? Who knows what Jack London actually heard? He was a great author whose mother was a mystic and Astrologer. In the starry arts the Moon symbolizes the mother, and the Valley of the Moon was where Jack made his *final home.* We're just lucky that he probably used some well-worn creative license to give us such a lovely name for this beautiful place.

Chapter Seven
The Imperial Russian River Story

Names are different from other words in the way that we accept them. We think of words as part of a sentence communicating an idea, like interdependent planets in their own Solar System, spinning around the Sunny subject and Lunar object. But names are like comets and islands, sovereign nations accepted at face value, with all their complicated history.

Consider the name *Chardonnay*, a popular white wine grape that appears on many menus and wine lists. People rarely wonder about that name's origin or meaning. They assume it's French, since the most famous representatives are from Burgundy and Champagne. Most people think the name means something in a local Patois and thus, like so much about the French countryside, its history is obscure and complicated, like *Merlot*, which means *blackbird*. But Chardonnay's name instead traces back to the Middle East, Syria, Lebanon and Israel where the grape was found by the Crusaders. In those languages the name Chardonnay means the *Gates of God*, which says much about the importance they ascribed to that pretty, luminous grape and its tremendously adaptable wine.

Coincidentally, Chardonnay is one of the two most popular grapes grown in the North Bay region whose names also have complicated and exotic histories. One of those is the *Russian River Valley*. People rarely ask us about the source of that name, yet we've lost count of the number of clients who were surprised that the Russians settled that green expanse north of San Francisco. Why else would they call that shallow, winding river that carries the silt and scent of the mountains all the way to the Pacific, the 'Russian' River? People just accept names without thinking, like New Yorkers accept the Russian Tearoom, formed by members of the Imperial Ballet, and the Russian Baths, started by a German physician in the 1800's, even though both Manhattan icons are far from Saint Petersburg.

Why would the Russians come to Northern California? Well, why wouldn't they? Russia's eastern coast is opposite Sonoma's, and the Russians are good at navigating ice, whether it's on the Baltic Sea, or the Pacific port of Vladivostok. That seaside city sits at the tip of the broad Siberian plateau, a place that Americans view as a great wasteland, but it's an area of huge resources.

Whenever there are things to sell and deep-water ports welcoming ships, there's commerce and Vladivostok is Russia's gateway to the Pacific rim and America's west coast.

It's easy to forget now that *Russia once controlled Alaska,* which it sold to the United States in 1867 for two cents an acre. At the time it was called Seward's Folly, for the Secretary of State who negotiated the sale. Considering the gold and oil Alaska contains, that turned out to be a good deal. For the Russians, exploiting Alaska was difficult because of the great distances and harsh weather. While the fur trade was very profitable, sustaining the colony was a Labor of Hercules, because transporting food from Western Russia to Alaska over the Trans-Siberian Railway was an *exercise in futility.*

If the food wasn't stolen by officials or brigands along the way, it rotted during the long rail trip and ensuing sea voyage. To feed their people it was decided to look in a different direction. The most practical was to the south along the Pacific coastline where there was warmer weather, so two ships were dispatched to find a suitable location for their settlement.

As the Russians sailed south, they knew that the land where they were planning to settle, had been claimed for England in the late 1600s by Sir Walter Raleigh when he was circumnavigating the globe in his ship, the Golden Hind. But Sir Walter did not hang around to protect his claim, poor guy.

While he did return to England to acclaim, with a ship full of treasure, he missed discovering the inlet to the San Francisco Bay by about ten miles. This is considered one of the world's greatest harbors, protected from the weather and fed by an extensive, navigable river system. This is exactly what sailors searched the globe for. Unfortunately for him, the inlet is hard to find from the ocean side. Sir Walter was so close, but no cigar!

Instead, they landed just north of the inlet on the marshy shores of Point Reyes. Then they passed by the outlet of the Russian River, but found it *too shallow* and filled with sand bars to navigate with a sailing ship. Finally, the Golden Hind moored in little Bodega Bay before setting out across the deep blue waters of the Pacific to the spice islands.

The Russians also knew that the Spanish had claimed parts of California as far north as San Francisco. This was the northern tip of their overextended empire before they ventured into Sonoma. The Spanish military was sorely lacking in the neighborhood, so it was difficult for them to protect their claim, but that doesn't mean a little diplomacy wasn't in order.

The Russian Governor met with the Spanish Commandant in Monterey to get his 'permission' for the settlement. It didn't hurt that the dashing Governor *fell in love* with the Commandant's beautiful daughter, but that's another, very romantic but dramatically sad story.

In 1812 the Russians tactfully found a spot along the California Coast in Sonoma, seventy miles north of the Spanish settlements in San Francisco. They held onto it for the next thirty years developing farms, orchards and ranches. Surely it was a pleasant change from the frozen north and their seal hunting camps in Alaska.

It didn't take long for them to realize how well they had chosen. While there's plenty of sunshine along the coast during the day, the nightly fog keeps the hillsides green for much of the year, making it an ideal place for raising food and grazing their livestock. While much of this region is prone to drought, that coastal band can get up to fifty inches of rain yearly.

Sonoma, with its many diverse climates, is such a 'Garden of Eden' that the famous botanist, Luther Burbank, who developed many of our popular fruit varieties, said that *of all the places on Earth he had visited, this was the 'most blessed by nature.'* Everything grows well there, whether it's native or not, from palm trees to apples, from grapes to redwoods. Burbank bought his farm in Santa Rosa in 1875 and built greenhouses where he did his research. Admittedly, it was about forty miles east of the Russia camp on the softly rolling hills and plains between the warmer Sonoma Valley and the cooler Russian River Valley.

The Russians built a fort with four strong walls and cannons, but they didn't have any soldiers, only traders, trappers and administrators. After discovering how difficult it was to hunt the sea otters that live along the California coast, they brought Aleut hunters, and their women, south from Kodiak Island in Alaska. The otter's coats are extremely dense and soft, and *there was a lucrative market for them among the Chinese royalty.*

While the hunters, with their kayaks, traveled along the coast in American sailing ships, the women farmed the land, producing the vegetables and fruits that were shipped up north. *It was a strange place and the Aleut women claimed that little 'people', the Irish would call them Leprechauns, would come out at night, running around the camp and causing mischief,* It was a pretty wild place during the day too.

Apparently, among the traders and trappers, a favorite diversion was getting drunk and firing the cannons. It happened so often that the settlement's bookkeeper complained about the expense for gun power. Today, when you go on the historic tour, one of the highlights is the firing of the cannon. We highly recommend a visit!

Where did the name Fort Ross come from? Who was this guy named Ross? There was no such person! In fact, *this is an example of 'California-ese,' a dialect similar to 'Spanglish,'* where words from different languages are married together. The English word 'Fort' is married to 'Ross,' which comes from the Russian word 'Rossiya,' which means 'Mother Russia.' The 'Russians,' actually included a wide variety of Eastern Europeans.

A wonderful example are the Bohemian brothers, from what is today modern Poland, who established the Korbel Winery on the cool Western edge of the Russian River Valley in the mid 1800's. Their historic winery buildings, situated just north of the river, are surrounded by their vineyards and coastal redwood forests.

The local tribes liked the Russians because they were honest in their trading and easy to work with. They were much preferred to the imperious and crafty Spanish, who sought to convert the local tribes to Christianity using the harshest methods possible, including kidnapping and virtual slavery. In a land where most of the westerners were a pretty wild group, the 'Russians' were culturally a pleasant contribution.

They were led by the handsome and talented Count Alexander Rotscheff, and his *beautiful*, highly refined wife, the Princess Ilona de Gagarin. They lived there with their three children and a surprising number of comforts, including musical instruments, but that's admittedly, another long story!

Russia held onto their Fort until it became clear that California was going to become part of the United States, at which point they sold it to John Sutter, of later gold rush fame. Why did they give up such a prime location? There were geopolitical reasons behind that choice! Their involvement in the Crimean War was causing them to withdraw resources from the Pacific, and they hoped that America controlling the area would suppress the British naval presence in the region. Britain was their main adversary.

Remember, the Russians sold Alaska to the United States, a deal for which Secretary of State Seward was roundly criticized. Who knew that thirty-one years later gold would be discovered there, starting the massive gold rush. Not only did it dramatically increase Alaska's population, but it made fortunes for the west coast shipping companies that connected the mines to San Francisco. While this is all very interesting, I heard the inside story from a wine tour client who was an American history professor teaching in Russia. Apparently, the Russians gave up their holdings in Alaska and California because they were afraid that their people would become infected with American Democracy!

Even though the Russians gave up their 'fort', there are many Bay Area families that trace their roots back to that settlement on the Sonoma Coast, where their ancestors just wanted a warm place to raise their food and children. Russian Hill in San Francisco takes its name from an old graveyard for those fur trappers. Later, when the Russian Revolution deposed the Czar, many of the aristocracy fled to the United States via the Pacific Port of Vladivostok.

When they arrived in San Francisco, they settled on *Russian Hill*. Early on, when I was researching this book, I was befriended by a tour guide who was raised in San Francisco, and he filled me in on much of the local color. He was a *direct descendant* of the Russian Governor of Alaska and proof that the heritage of 'Fort Rossiya' lives on in the Bay Area.

Opposite: Ferrari-Carano Vineyards

Chapter Eight
Wine Country's Great Buildings

Wine Country has a wonderful collection of winery buildings. The first were built in the early 1800s, and many of those are still in use today. The builders began by using redwood, either found on the site, or brought from the towering forests that blanket the Pacific Coast. Even though those beautiful, red boards stand up well to bugs and rot, they are not as durable as stone. So, in the late 1800's the builders turned to masonry, which has long been considered the ideal material for a winery.

Stone is perfect for a building which needs to stay cool and humid while standing up to water and the acids found in wine. Starting in the 1970's there was an influx of international companies building dramatic wineries where the architecture would add to the attraction.

But when the Spanish first arrived in the North Bay, they just needed to make wine.

The region's first prominent winemaker was a native '*Californio*' and Spanish officer, General Mariano Guadalupe Vallejo, born in Monterey on July 4th, a date of which he was particularly proud due its affinity with the United States. Mariano produced wine under his label, 'Lachryma Montis,' or '*the Tears of the Mountain,*' named for the spring above his home in Sonoma. It was from his vineyards that *George Yount, mountain man and wagon train leader,* purchased the first grape vines planted in the heart of the Napa Valley. Yount's Caymus Spring Ranch was a grant from the General.

Those early winemakers planted high sugar Mission grapes and fermented them in tanks made from cow hides hung on a frame. But they soon learned from the winemakers who came there from Hungary, Prussia, France and Italy, who were well aware of the advantages that wooden tanks and stone buildings provided to the winemaker. The General's most obvious contributions to the local architecture are the historic buildings around the Plaza, and two notable houses, built in New England and transported by sailing ship to Sonoma, one for his home and another for his daughter.

The development of a winemaking region happens in stages, often over many generations. But Napa and Sonoma gained a great head start in the 1800s, thanks to a stream of cheap labor from Italy and China arriving through the Golden Gate. Italy's winemaking tradition predates the Romans, and in the 1800's it was their dominant industry. But the combination of diseased vines and drought sent thousands of young Italian men streaming to America in search of related work. In San Francisco, Chinese labor contractors would provide as many workers as a vineyard owner could afford. They did the backbreaking work of clearing the land and stacking the stones into long border walls that you can still see today.

They also dug the earliest *wine caves*. Later they built the dikes and levees that allowed thousands of acres of land along the edges of the bay to be reclaimed for farming, coincidentally eliminating the malarial marshes that once covered a third of the bay. The lines of fragrant *eucalyptus trees* that you see by the bay were part of that strategy. They pull a great deal of water out of the ground and the scent discourages the mosquitos. You still find old ranch houses in Los Carneros surrounded by orderly groves of tall, graceful eucalyptus.

Buena Vista Winery

Count Agoston Haraszthy built two of California's first stone winery buildings at Buena Vista in Sonoma in 1857. He was a great believer in the Chinese workers who cleared his vineyards and dug his caves. The *'Colonel,'* as he was respectfully known locally, was a contemporary and friend of General Vallejo, to whom he was eventually related through the marriage of their children. Two of the Count's sons married two of the General's daughters. Haraszthy's two winery buildings are still in use today, which is a story in itself.

The buildings were damaged by a series of earthquakes, but the smaller of the two, used for brandy making, was repaired with *earthquake stars*. Those are the threaded endcaps that appear on the outside of the building when a steel rod has been installed to prevent the walls from spreading.

Often with these old buildings in an earthquake prone area, a veritable constellation will dot the outside. Today the brandy building serves as the tasting room, with a small museum upstairs. The larger of the two was the main winemaking building, but the damage it sustained was more challenging to repair, so it sat *unused* for many years while the winery went through several owners.

Finally in 2011 the new owner, Jean-Charles Boisset, began an extensive restoration. When the work was finished, wine was once again being produced in the grand building, more than 160 years after the first stones were laid. The remainder of the three-story building is devoted to hospitality spaces, including a wine tool museum and, of course, offices! The most remarkable part of that story was the way it was restored. Instead of depending on 'earthquake stars,' an expedient, yet sometimes ugly solution, they took a more expensive and demanding approach.

They removed the roof and drilled holes through the entire height of the stone walls and into the foundation. Then they placed *steel rods* inside the holes and filled them with epoxy, creating a new superstructure inside the walls. Today, visitors enjoy the winery that looks very much like it did when the Count was still walking on these grounds, talking about making his great wines in California.

As compared to Napa where there are more 'destination' wineries, Sonoma's tradition is bucolic and homey. One of its iconic houses from the 1920's is the white mansion on the Chateau Saint Jean property. Today it is used for winery hospitality, but it started as a home for a wealthy Midwestern family. By today's standards it is not big, but it is gracious and beautifully appointed, paneled with exotic woods and designed to take advantage of the views.

The family and the great botanist Luther Burbank were friends, and the beautiful gardens continue to reflect a love of gardening. It faces east and spreads out in a long line from north to south. On the west side, the two wings extend out to form a protected courtyard, perfect for watching the setting sun. On the southside *there once was a pond shaped* like the Great Lakes to remind them of their home in the Midwest.

Jordan Vineyard & Winery

In Northern Sonoma's Alexander Valley you will find the Jordan Winery, completed in 1979. It is a grand *chateau* in the French style, that stretches along the top of a hill, at the end of a long, curving drive. On one end are the offices. In the middle is the dramatic winery with its tall wooden tanks that had to be lowered into place before the roof was installed. At the other end are luxurious apartments for the wine club members. They face a spacious, hedge trimmed patio to relax on, with a glass of wine while you enjoy the view of the vineyard cascading down the slopes.

At the top of Northern Sonoma's Dry Creek Valley sits the very elaborate Ferrari-Carano Winery, with its beautiful gardens. This was built by the Carano family, starting in the early 1980's. They own casinos in Reno Nevada, and there may be a touch of that in its flamboyant style, because most of Northern Sonoma is pretty 'country'. The property has a *dual personality* because the two main buildings, one for winemaking and the other for hospitality, were built in two quite different styles. Aesthetically this seems odd to someone accustomed to the homogeneous nature of European wineries.

In Bordeaux, the great chateaus all share a similar look. In Italy, the grand villas follow traditional lines. But the long, rambling winery building at Ferrari-Carano is distinctly Japanese, which is funny since that country's winemaking tradition for centuries was primarily Saki.

When the Carano family built their impressive hospitality center in an elaborate Italianate manner and placed it on a scenic rise, opposite the winery. When you emerge from behind the hedge that separates the property from the parking lot, you see the elaborate, Italian style building on a rise at the end of a long walkway, bordered by a picture-perfect lawn. The building is not parallel to the walkway, or the winery, but canted inward so as you approach you can clearly see the front at an attractive angle.

Along the right side of the lawn is a high wall concealing a beautiful ornamental garden that incorporates both Asian and western motifs. You enter the garden just steps from the parking lot and emerge, thoroughly charmed by Mrs. Carano magical garden right before the building, bypassing the pathway.

Napa Makes a Change in the 1800's

Fortunately for the Napa winemakers, when they wanted to build their wineries in the late 1800's, Sonoma was awash in Italian immigrants, a culture with an ancient masonry tradition. Because Sonoma is so similar to Piedmont, Italy, boatloads of young Italian men came there looking for work. At that time the cheapest berth on a steamer was equivalent to a long-distance bus ticket today. Italy is a mountainous country blessed with abundant quarries of marble, granite, and alabaster, so the profession of mason is more common than that of carpenter. In Italy a wood parquet floor is considered a greater luxury than the more common marble.

Wine Country was not the only beneficiary of this migratory event. The wonderful stone buildings that grace our *Ivy League Universities* were built by Italian masons, whose descendants often still live in those towns. Most of America's stone churches and the most ornate of Washington DC's government buildings owe their stately beauty to those anonymous Italian stone masons and sculptors.

No matter how much an architect tries to impose their design style on a building, the people who use their hands to build it always get a vote. In downtown Napa the Italian craftsmen's influence on a very non-Italian building, is there for everyone to see. The historic Presbyterian Church on Third and Randolph was built in 1889. Traditionally, American Presbyterian churches are simpler than the elaborate Catholic Churches.

Yet this towering wooden building is dramatic, with its big stained-glass windows, and most notably, numerous figures adorning the outside, very much in the Roman Catholic style. Why? Because Italian craftsmen built it, and in their eyes, a church *needed statues of the Saints* adorning the exterior to welcome the congregation. More than likely the supervising architect was busy with another project, and by the time he came back the workers were putting away their tools and heading to another job site. Any changes cost extra!

Successful buildings need to stand up to the prevailing weather, even in California's lovely Mediterranean climate that is so kind to humans, grapes and olives. Visitors from colder climes are often surprised to hear that the mountaintops lining the valleys get traces of snow every few winters, like *the dusting of sugar* on top of an almond croissant from our famous bakeries. The Northern Italian masons seemed to have missed that point because they built substantial structures prepared to endure hundreds of years of rain, ice and snow, even though we don't do that kind of weather here!

That does explain why these great stone structures still look so good after twelve decades, despite having endured multiple earthquakes and thirty to forty years of abandonment due to Prohibition. Admittedly the mason's propensity to overbuild was thoroughly supported by the Vermont born, and New England trained architect and winery engineer Hamden McIntyre. He had built wineries in the Finger Lakes region of New York State and worked as a marine engineer in Canada and

Alaska. When the first stone wineries were being imagined McIntyre was working in San Francisco. He had come to California to help re-organize a newly formed shipping partnership, Hansen, Nybom and Company.

The youngest partner, whom *Hamden* befriended, was *Captain Gustave Niebaum,* a Finnish American ship captain who made a fortune shipping furs from Alaska. Gustave eventually changed the Finnish spelling of his name Nybom, to the German spelling in deference to his German Jewish partners.

As Niebaum grew increasingly wealthy, he dreamed of outfitting a ship and sailing the world with his beloved German American wife, and then buying a French Chateau. But Suzanne, born in California, didn't like boats, hated the ocean and didn't want to live in France, so far from her home. Instead, they decided to build Napa's first grand winery, naming it Inglenook, which they call a small, cozy seating nook, big enough for two, alongside a fireplace.

They built a Victorian mansion at the foot of the Mayacamas mountains in Rutherford, *with a carriage house where the captain made his first wine.* Gustave traveled throughout Europe as far east as Hungry, to observe wine making techniques. He brought back a wide variety of grape vines he planted in their vineyards, including many that are popular today. While Gustave and Suzanne Niebaum never had children, they adopted his wife's niece and nephew and raised them as their own.

In an interesting case of history repeating itself, many years later when the Coppola's bought the house.

Francis made his first wine in that same carriage house and called it Rubicon. As you might recall from Roman history, the Rubicon River was the northern border between Gaul and Italy. When Julius Caesar came back from his triumphant five years in what is today's modern France, his enemies in the Senate planned to ruin him in the courts. To save his honor he led a small portion of his army across the river, the official border of Italy, which made him a rebel. His famous quote as they road into the water was, *"Let the dice fly high."*

His enemies were so terrified by his approach that they abandoned the city, and the treasury stuffed with gold and he because the virtual ruler of Rome. By naming the wine Rubicon, they were saying that now that they made their first wine, there was no turning back.

But back to Niebaum's marvelous building. The captain wanted to build a state-of-the-art winery in Napa, thousands of miles from France so he engaged an architect who understood the aesthetics of a classic building. But he was not familiar with gravity fed wineries. Fortunately, McIntyre had been trained in winemaking and knew all about wineries, so he came on as the project's general manager.

That's not to say that the Captain wasn't deeply involved in creating the winery. *His agents throughout Europe continued to send him books* on the latest advances in winemaking methods and technology, and these were incorporated into the building and winery processing.

The Inglenook Winery design was such a success that Hamden McIntyre spent many years designing some of Napa's most famous winery buildings. Considering that Hamden's original training included wooden New England style buildings, it's said that only two of his local redwood wineries remain. The first is the winemaking barn at Frog's Leap in Rutherford, with its jaunty leaping frog weathervane. *Their slogan is, "Time's fun when you're having flies."* The other is the classic, three story Eschol winery, today owned by the Trefethen family, at the corner of Saint Helena Highway and Oak Knoll, surrounded by their five-hundred-acre vineyard.

The story goes that it was McIntyre's favorite and that his ghost haunts it. However, that's pretty unlikely. Not that it's haunted, wine country has plenty of ghosts. But it's not McIntyre, because even though he was in high demand for his winery designs, Hamden and Susan moved back to Vermont where he stayed productive, although not building his wonderful wineries.

If you love buildings, please visit the Trefethen winery, because it is a wonderful example of the New England woodworker's art with its massive beams and classic joints. Another example is the red barn at the Nickel and Nickel property in Oakville. Built in the 1700's, *it was disassembled and transported to the estate where it was carefully reassembled.*

I've walked though many of these classic barns and I thought I knew a bit about them, but then the director of Napa's Historical Society filled in a fascinating connection. The wood joints that hold the classic New England barns together *are the same designs as those used on sailing ships of the period.* How did that happen? Simple, the same craftsman built both barns and ships, moving back and forth between the country and the coast with the seasons.

This combination of well-traveled European investors, sturdy northern Italian stonemasons and a New England winery engineer resulted in a collection of wineries that often resemble fortresses, like Far Niente, Chateau Montelena, Greystone and many more. These grand structures are interspersed with dozens of smaller stone buildings from that period. This was the *last great expression* of the traditional builders' art that had developed over the centuries. As the twentieth century dawned, natural stone was eclipsed by steel, aluminum, plywood and sheet rock.

In 1919 Prohibition began and most of the winery buildings were abandoned. Even though it ended thirteen years later, many growers had shifted to other crops. It wasn't until the 1970s, when there were more orchards than vineyards in the valley, that the interest in growing premium wine grapes locally was revived. That's when investors began looking at these great structures and imagining the possibilities.

One of the hidden advantages that often made the expense of renovation worthwhile was an idiosyncrasy of the winery regulations. It's much easier legally to establish a new winery on a site where a previous one had operated, even if just one corner of that building remains.

When building in California, one must always consider the effects of *earthquakes*, because they will eventually happen! One of the more interesting stories

I heard is about our dear Inglenook. After the devastating 6.9 Loma Prieta earthquake, that shook the 1989 World Series, engineers examined public buildings to determine how to make them safe. They were followed by tradesmen with bolts, straps and steel to stop structures from being knocked off their foundations, or crumbling.

The main building at Inglenook is an impressive pile of stone quarried from the property, along with a significant amount poured concrete. It is three stories tall, sitting on thick walls, cut by narrow windows, with a series of arched chambers on the first floor to store wine barrels.

As is common with gravity fed wineries like Far Niente and Graystone, Inglenook is built into a hillside. That allowed grape wagons to drive up the low hill behind the winery to the level of the very solid second floor. There men would unload bins of grapes into the fermentation tanks. Finally, when the yeast had turned the juice into wine, a hose was attached to the tank and run down to the first floor. They would open the valve and fill the empty aging barrels without needing a pump. This was important in the days before electric and pneumatic pumps were commonplace. In those days moving juice required either a siphon and buckets, or a manual pump with a long handle and a *strong arm.*

Because Inglenook's concrete second story was so substantial, McIntyre knew it made the upper building heavy, so he planned for that. The masons embedded old trolley car cables into the wet concrete of that thick, second floor. The ends were *anchored into the*

Inglenook Winery

hillside, to prevent the earthquakes, that would surely come from breaking up Inglenook's tight embrace of its hillside. Today, the building and grounds enjoy an abundance of care and it's surely worth the visit. As the engineers inspected the building, they were amazed that it didn't suffer any structural damage in the quake."

A *horrible* example of what a quake can do was Trefethen's wooden winery. The 2014 Napa quake happened during harvest, and even though the wooden building no longer operates as a gravity fed winery, they had wine barrels, filled with water, on the second floor preparing to accept new wine. It made the building top heavy enough to magnify the quake's effects.

The result that I saw driving up the valley was a building leaning over about four feet. Those huge one hundred-and twenty-year-old redwood beams had bent but not broken. That great building never let go of its foundation.

Trefethen Family Vineyards

When they started the restoration, they attached cables to the upright beams and anchored them to the foundation at the back of the building. They planned to do a *'chiropractic adjustment,'* cranking the cables tighter and tighter until the building stood straight. They were hoping to get an inch of movement a day, but on the first day those big beams flexed, and the building stood right up, within inches of its original position. After the family's herculean efforts, it is still greeting visitors today.

The Far Niente Winery was built at the same time and also into a small knoll, with two driveways running up the hill to the two upper floors. Today, when you visit the winery, the very top floor is a charming reception area, with a long table for guests and windows that look east over the vineyards. The building was the work of the Italian masons who carved the words *'Far Niente'* into the lintel above the planned cave entrance, that were dug almost ninety years later. Those words are a fragment of the winery's original name, 'In Dolce Far Niente,' which itself is a shortened version of the original Italian expression, "Il dolce piacere per far niente," meaning *'the sweet pleasure of doing nothing.'*

For men who worked daily with blocks of stone, hammers, chisels and hand cranked cranes, their leisure time must have been especially sweet. The building sat empty for many years, but not entirely due to prohibition. During that unfortunate period when making wine was illegal, a wealthy widow lived in the home with her young and dashing second husband, who had been a World War One flying Ace. He built an *airstrip* on the property and routinely smuggled liquor out of the valley in his airplane. His entrepreneurial venture came to an unfortunate end when his wife's daughter, who had no affection for her stepfather, poisoned him!

After that, the joy pretty much went out of the home, and it sat empty for many years. When the current owners, the Nickel family, took it over in the 1970's they found that the structure was so well built that the main task, prior to installing the new systems, was removing the trees and bushes that had overtaken the property in the ensuing years. *Then they dug the caves.*

Not every stone building from that era was so fortunate. At the top of the valley at the northern edge of the town of Saint Helena, a very long and tall building called Greystone towers over the road. It was once the home of the Christian Brothers Cellars, but thanks to the Loma Prieta earthquake, it is now the west coast home of The Culinary Institute of America.

The Culinary Institute of America at Greystone

Unlike Inglenook and Far Niente, which were built into knolls on the settled valley floor, Greystone was built into an unstable hillside in the narrowest part of the valley. This is where the western slope of the volcanic Vaca Mountains *almost touches* the eastern slope of the Mayacamas Mountains, that in this part of the valley contains a great deal of volcanic ash. The two ranges form a mile wide neck on the bottom-heavy hourglass shape that describes the Napa Valley.

The hillside is so steep that Greystone's parking lot sits high above the road, where a long flight of steep stairs brings you up to the first floor. At the back of that ground floor, Chinese workers had dug a wine cave that went deep into the hillside. Inside the central entranceway, multiple open staircases wind their way up to the top floor where the cooking school now resides. This

complex balancing act of leaning against the hill and de-
fying gravity worked well for many years, *until* the Loma
Prieta earthquake gave those ashy hillsides a serious
shaking.

At the time, the Christian Brothers had been making wine there for many years and aging it in the caves
below. As an aside, in case you're wondering whether
these are natural caves, while in the long history of winemaking, natural caves have been employed, the caves in
the north bay were, and continue to be dug by industrious miners.

After the quake, the inherent instability that ex-
isted on that hillside made itself known. It required an
extensive amount of work to prevent the building's walls
from heading off in different directions. This required
the installation of a constellation of *'earthquake stars'*
that can be seen on the front of the building. They serve
as the end nuts for steel rods that span the building and
connect the front and back walls together, preventing
them from spreading apart.

The place where this instability was most obvious
was in the dirt below, where the cave was located. It was
also the place that would be the hardest and most expensive to fix, because there's an awful lot of unstable stone
on top of those caves and gravity is undeniable. For the
Christian Brothers this was a disaster because having a
cool, humid cave to age their wine was essential.

Eventually, Christian Brothers decided to move to
another facility and the building was sold to the Culinary
Institute of America *for a dollar*, with the

acceptance that it was up to the new owners to do the required repairs. Fortunately, the CIA, as it's known locally, was looking for a West Coast location.

Sonoma was also in the running, but the Greystone property was a good solution for them for an odd reason. They were one of the few potential buyers in the heart of Wine Country that wasn't a winery, so they didn't care about the condition of the caves.

While the 'earthquake stars' on the exterior can be mistaken for decorations, inside the north part of the building that is less supported by the hill, there is so much structural steel arching through the rooms that you feel like you're standing inside the upper parts of the Brooklyn Bridge.

That part of the Valley, on the edge of the little town of Saint Helena, is also home to Napa's oldest winery, Charles Krug. It was started on land that was part of his wife's dowry. Charles had worked for the Count over in Sonoma as a winemaker, before he started his own winery, which he owned for a short time. But the ensuing owners built two remarkable stone buildings, one for the winery and an expansive carriage house that today is used for events.

The Mondavi family came north from the Central Valley after WWII and bought the winery and ran it as a family affair. After the famous feud between the two brothers, Robert took his share and started his own winery, and Peter's family has continued to make their wines there in a modern, solar powered building. The historic winery is used for aging barrels and hospitality. One of Krug's employees was fellow Prussian, Jacob Beringer.

While Jacob worked at Krug, his brother in New York was raising money, and eventually they bought the land across the street and started the Beringer Brothers Winery in 1876. The stone winery buildings were tucked against the hill so they could dig caves in the back. Their most remarkable architectural contribution was their Rhine House. To build it Jacob moved a spacious, California style home to the north where it is surrounded by a lovely grove of redwood trees. This way his emblematic building would stand out prominently just inside the gate. The Rhine House was based on their childhood home in Prussia, so the fish and birds portrayed in the stained-glass windows are those breeds found *near their ancestral home.* The dining room windows include food themes, the drawing room tea and beverages.

This impressively beautiful building was one of Napa's first great 'castles'. Today the mansion that was once their home is used for pouring their most expensive wines, while the old winery building is used for the rest of the list. The wines are made across the road, outside in an orderly collection of stainless-steel tanks you can see as you drive by on Saint Helena Highway.

Another contemporary winery in that neighborhood is on the road up to Spring Mountain. It was built buy a *Monsieur Parrot,* the French son of Captain Gustave Niebaum's business partner in their wildly successful shipping company. It includes an impressive hillside cave fronted by a dramatic steeple.

He and his wife were planning their home just after Jacob Beringer had completed his dramatic Rhine House, that was turning everyone's head. For Monsieur and Madame Parrot, it was a daunting task trying to keep up with the Berringer's' love of expensive, decorative woods and stained glass, *so they took a simpler route.* Parrot simply told their architect, 'We don't care what it looks like so much, as long as it's taller than the Beringer's house,' and it is!

In an interesting Hollywood twist, the house was used in the 1980's 'nighttime soap opera' Falcon Crest, about wealthy families of wine country. The intro featured the image of a falcon from one of the house's stained-glass windows. In the true spirit of Hollywood, the part of *the titular Falcon shown in the window, was played by a parrot,* the namesake of the family Parrot!

The same masons that built the wineries laid the blocks and bricks for many of the charming storefront buildings in downtown Saint Helena and Napa. Those materials set them apart from downtown Sonoma on the other side of the Mayacamas Mountains. There you'll find a wonderful collection of adobe buildings constructed during the Spanish colonial period, with their soft, rounded edges, enclosing courtyards and paseos, shielded from the heat. The main reason that Sonoma never replaced the buildings was money, there is no river nearby so there was less commerce. But, because downtown Sonoma lacked a river, they didn't suffer from Napa's devastating floods, so they simply repaired the buildings they had, including the historic Mission and the Presidio Barracks.

In comparison, the Napa River promoted so much commercial activity, and the downtown was so subject to floods, that the owners could afford to tear down the single-story, mud adobes and replace them with more durable, multi-story stone buildings, in the early 1900's. The only historic Napa adobe was beautifully restored and today is home to a restaurant south of downtown Napa. It was the home of the original Mexican settler and his family, Sergeant Nicolás Higuera, who had received a massive land grant from his commander, General Vallejo. His ranchero included what is today downtown Napa and a large part of Los Carneros.

In 2014 the Napa Quake destructively shook the downtown, where massive stone blocks flew off the fronts of the turn of the century buildings. In Sonoma, even though the quake burst the wine tanks at the downtown Sebastiani winery, the historic adobes came through it with just a few cracks. Rebuilding downtown Napa was a lengthy process because those Italian stone masons are long gone, and today fewer people possess those remarkable and enduring skills.

Today the masons are still mostly immigrants, and they continue to build remarkable structures. One of the most beautiful modern wineries in Napa is Darioush. It is constructed from golden travertine marble quarried in Iran and milled and carved in Italy and Turkey. It is patterned on the ancient Persian capital *Persepolis*. I also heard that it was based on *Heliopolis*, the temple of the Sun, which seems suitable considering the material and design.

It is a beautifully balanced building, with a large complex cave underneath. The center front section is for hospitality, while the left wing is their office. The winery is at the back and separated by a glass wall. The right wing is a home. Outside at the north side of the building is an amphitheater, where the upper rows are at ground level, and the bottom is at the same level as the cave floor. The front of the building faces west, but the draining effects of the afternoon sun are mitigated by the rich colors of the materials.

As you approach Darioush columns mimic a line of trees, topped with sculptures of horses. On either side are ponds with water flowers. In the center is a sunken area with steps down to the paved floor. This is a seating area that I've only seen used once. It was filled with low, Persian cushions, and an off-white cloth was draped over the tops of the columns to provide shade, making it an amazingly appealing space.

For all the chateaus, villas and mansions that populate the North Bay, the Castello di Amorosa in Northern Napa has the greatest right to the title, 'Castle,' because it was patterned on Tuscan Medieval castles. The person who dreamed this up was Dario Sattui, of the long-time V. Sattui Winery. Thanks to its location in a commercial zone, instead of the restrictive Agricultural Preserve, V. Sattui is able to have a deli with picnic tables. When I started wine touring in 2005, one out of every eight Napa visitors tasted at V. Sattui and then had lunch there.

After a good run Dario was semi-retired, spending half his time in Italy. But back in Napa Valley he bought a hillside vineyard behind a large house just south of downtown Calistoga that he planned to turn into a Bed and Breakfast. The next part of the story is a bit of my speculation about how the idea for a castle winery in Napa came about. About the time when he was living in Tuscany, a local family was building a winery styled as a castle. You could see it from the Autostrada, along with a very tall, turquoise crane.

The idea of creating a destination winery in Tuscany was quite a departure. Italy has half a million wineries and the place is practically carpeted in vineyards, so having a winery in your neighborhood is about as common as having a bakery. It must have got Dario thinking, "If they can build a castle winery in Tuscany, why can't I build one in Napa?" so he did!

He had architects create plans of various Tuscan castles and then they got together and created a new design. They built an authentic hundred and seven room, eight level high stone castle, using tons of building materials, including wrought iron and carvings from Italy.

He named it Castello Di Amorosa, or 'Castle of the Beloved.' Was it a good bet? I was there two weeks after it opened, when I hadn't seen a single advertisement for it yet, and they were already *booked to capacity*. Another time I dropped by with my daughter and Disney was shooting the movie 'Bedtime Story' starring Adam Sandler.

For that they finally filled the moat with water and in return the crew built an impressive Medieval village that extended from the front path to the drawbridge and into the courtyard. But even during filming, the tasting room downstairs stayed open.

El Castello is *one of three destination wineries within sight of its parapets.* The original star of the upper valley was Sterling, opening their white, Greek, Mykonos Island style winery on the top of a hill in the 1970's. It features a tramway to carry visitors from the parking lot up to the winery with its splendid views. Sterling was the first winery to charge for tastings, although you could say that the guests paid for the tram ride, and once they arrived at the top the wines were free.

Just across the street from the entrance to Sterling is Clos Pegase. Traditionally, Clo in the name of a French winery means a walled, or enclosed vineyard. Clo Pegase was originally home to a wonderful sculpture collection, inside of a *delightfully colorful Michael Graves designed building.* Being able to taste their wines while surrounded by this wonderful collection of art was a unique experience. Periodically they had artists in residence who would use the tank room as their studio and gallery. But things change. Clos Pegase was sold, and the art collection departed with the owner.

For some unknown and ill-informed reason, the new *owners painted that beautiful, uniquely colored building a remarkably boring gray.* So, while Clo Pegase continues to make good wines, the draw for art and architecture is gone.

Then, in 2020 the North Napa fire burned massive tracts above downtown Saint Helena, forcing part of the town's evacuation. The fire raged up Howell

Mountain and the firebrands blew across the valley onto Spring Mountain. The fires destroyed dozens of winery buildings, homes and even some steep hillside vineyards. While most of the vineyards weren't touched by the fires, smoke damage tainted the grapes still on the vines so badly that they became unusable. *The fire climbed Sterling's steep hilltop,* destroying many of the trees that had once shaded the buildings and leaving burn marks on the outside of the winery.

Fortunately, it did not go up in flames, although it destroyed the popular tramway, which was the only way to bring customers to the top. It took until October of 2023 for Sterling to reopen. After being part of a dynamic trio of destination wineries at the top of the valley, suddenly the Castello found itself the sole star in that constellation. That was true even though the hills surrounding it were covered with charred tree stumps, and their large storage building, filled with wine, was gutted by the fire. However, they got their doors open to visitors after that disaster remarkably fast. There is an advantage to being in a traditional stone building.

From the road El Castello sits hidden, on the far side of an impressive gate, up a long, steep, curving lane lined with trees and vines. As you approach, the building suddenly appears, a towering pile of stone at the top of the hill. An orchard of hundred-year-old Italian olive trees, and grazing sheep surround the building. The architecture includes some whimsical grace notes. A favorite of mine are the small 'repair' bricks that were fit into 'damaged' addition that juts out over the eastern entrance to the cellar. There are also the bricked up 'old' doorways and crumbling towers that you expect to see in a Medieval Castle. It makes the statement that, *'Yes, we've taken hits and it's been hard, but we adapted to the times, and we are still here!'*

Castello di Amorosa

Chapter Nine
Sonoma and Napa, Ancient Siblings

Understanding the relationship between Sonoma and Napa is like recognizing the connections between siblings. I imagine Sonoma as the older sister, dark-haired, good looking, industrious, a great cook and gardener and always responsible. Meanwhile, Napa is her golden-haired little brother that everyone makes a fuss over. Whenever he shows up carrying a basket of grapes, or a bottle of wine, everybody turns around and looks at him smiling. It drives his older sister crazy, even though she knows that he adores her.

People visiting often assume there must be competition between the two regions. After all, these are *two of the world's most popular wine destinations* with respected international reputations and markets. A big part of their tourism success *stems from them being conveniently close to San Francisco,* itself a long-time tourist and convention destination. Because the North Bay Wine Country was a popular day trip from the city, their fame spread until they eventually became destinations themselves.

Surprisingly, there's little competition between the two, although maybe a little friendly rivalry, for a very good reason. Even though they are both wine growing regions, they produce wines from mostly different grapes. That is a function, as is always the case in natural agriculture, of location. California's western border is the Pacific Ocean, and that massive body of frigid water shapes almost everything about grape growing in the state.

The closer you are to the ocean, the cooler the temperatures. Because the North Bay wine region is divided up by hills and mountains, running north to south, *each valley you cross, going east from the ocean, is warmer.* There are thousands of grape varieties world-wide, and they all have specific climates to which they are most adapted, so as you travel east from Sonoma to Napa, the varieties that thrive change.

There is no ignoring the reality that the two countries that most influenced winemaking in California are France and Italy. But here we come to a paradox. The most popular, successful and prestigious wines made in California come from grapes that originated in France. Yet, much of the labor and entrepreneurship that created the wine industry in America came from Italian immigrants. They initially planted vines that produced wines that tasted familiar and coincidentally, ripened early, such as Zinfandel, originally from Croatia, Grenache, from Spain via southern France, and the French varietals Alicante Bouchet and Petite Sirah. Over time, their popularity was supplanted by the French Chardonnay and Cabernet Sauvignon, the world's two most widely planted premium grapes. In Napa and Sonoma, where they grow California's most expensive wines knowing what to plant can be challenging.

Because it takes so long for the vines to mature and produce good grapes, growers need to forecast the market, and that means taking risks. But farmers are typically risk *averse*, which makes them resistant to change. You can always tell the serious grape growers in the area by their gray hair, from worrying about what the weather gods are going to do to their vines each year. The barometer they often watch are the grape varietals that are selling well in the fine restaurants, where many customers first encounter premium wines, because that's what they will look for in the future!

In France, Chardonnay and Pinot Noir are grown in the cool northeast regions of Burgundy and Champagne. Cabernet blends are grown in the warmer southwest region of Bordeaux. north of the San Francisco Bay, the relationship between France's northeast and southwest becomes the difference between cool Western Sonoma and warm Eastern Napa. While Burgundy and Bordeaux are hundreds of miles apart, the ride from Sonoma to Napa is just a twenty-minute drive over the wooded

Mayacamas Mountains. There is a California saying that is a truism, *"If you don't like the weather, just drive twenty minutes."*

Sonoma is almost three times larger than Napa and the two are topographically separated by the broad Mayacamas Mountains. There is only one relatively level road connecting them. It's called the Carneros Highway, and it stretches across the rolling hills just north of San Pablo Bay, which is what they call the northern reaches of the San Francisco Bay. Most of the road is wonderfully flat, except for *one big hill* at the county line. That steep ridge is the southernmost tip of the Mayacamas Mountains.

Today, for the modern traveler in an air-conditioned car listening to their music, the crest of the hill is a pleasant announcement that they've arrived in the next county, but in the days of *horse drawn wagons, teamsters surely dreaded that climb.* They couldn't build the road further south, where the land is flatter, because it would have skirted the malarial marshes and been prone to flooding. Further to the west in Sonoma the lower part of the road often floods in the Winter, even though the border of the bay has been pushed back behind grasslands protected by levies.

Napa is one wide valley, with vineyards carpeting the floor in some places and then extending up into the surrounding hills and canyons. Sonoma is made up of numerous valleys, large and small, that each create their own unique climates. Sonoma vineyards tend to be tucked in between forests, orchards, farms and towns.

To the west of the Sonoma Valley, over a low line of hills, alongside a river is the cooler, and very hip town of Petaluma. *The name means 'low hills' in the native language.* That small distance makes a difference. Sitting in the Sonoma Plaza on a bright morning with a cup of coffee, we would often see clouds hanging in the west, and comment, "Ah, it's cloudy in Petaluma." Whenever we drive there it's not quite as bright and warm as downtown Sonoma.

Farther west, beyond a wide plain, is the final line of steep hills beyond which are the cool waters of the Pacific. This is Sonoma's coastal region where they grow many of the most prized pinot noir grapes, and graze cattle on hills that stay green through much of the year.

Sonoma, with its complex geology and multitude of climates, can successfully grow a wider selection of grapes than Napa. While it's most famous for Pinot Noir and Chardonnay from the Russian River Valley and Los Carneros, it shines in other areas too.

Sonoma Valley, which thanks to its proximity to San Francisco, has long been a popular tourist destination, is a magical place that seems to be able to do a good job of growing every kind of local grape well. *Little Bennett Valley, which branches off to the west from the Sonoma Valley, produces some of the state's best Syrah.*

Northern Sonoma's Dry Creek Valley is famous for its Zinfandel. Next door, the Alexander Valley, with its broad floor at the foot of the eastern slopes of the Mayacamas Mountains, enjoys big sun and cool nights, much like Napa. Alexander Valley grows similar varietals on a different geology, so their Merlot is more muscular, and the Cabernet Sauvignon is milder. This is the home of *Geyser Peak,* that for years spewed steam from its cone. This area was actively volcanic ten thousand years ago, not long in geological time. It makes the charming town of Geyserville subject to daily, but minor tremors. Being in this perpetual state of flux gives it the feeling of a dusty old western town, that happens to have great restaurants, cool tasting rooms and a friendly cafe.

Unlike so many Spanish named cities in California, Sonoma and Napa's names spring from the native languages. This speaks volumes about the prosperity of this place where the native tongues had no word for starvation. The region directly north of the bay is one of the longest continually inhabited regions in North America, and that continuity promotes great culture. *The Sonoma tribes were famous storytellers and revered for their knowledge of plants. The Napa tribes were skilled craftspeople and their obsidian knives,* arrowheads and grinding boards were valuable assets to tribes throughout the west.

In the traditions of exploration, the fact that Sonoma was developed before Napa is an anomaly. Napa has the great advantage of being accessible by a navigable river, which should have tilted the odds in their favor. But the Spanish empire's resources were stretched to the breaking point in the 1800's, and they didn't have ships to spare for exploring the bay's complex network of rivers. That's because their galleons were sailing from the coast of Mexico, on the prevailing southern currents, *across the Pacific to the Philippines for the very profitable spice trade.* On their return, riding the northern currents, they would make landfall on the Alta California coast, and then follow that south to their base in Mexico. They would stay far out to sea to avoid the fog and the treacherous currents along the shore. With so much wealth at stake they wouldn't risk their cargo just to explore some wild place at the ends of the Earth.

While the Commandant in Monterey didn't have command of ships, he did have soldiers and horses. So, the way that the Spanish reached Sonoma was by crossing the Golden Gate inlet in boats and walking north for several days. The other route that they used when moving horses required a long ride east, staying south of the marshes, to where they could ford the Sacramento River, followed by a long ride west to Sonoma.

On the eve of the Bear Flag Rebellion in 1846, when California declared itself an independent Republic on the Sonoma Plaza in front of the barracks, this route played a critical role. When the Bear Flaggers arrived in Sonoma the General had no soldiers handy to confront them. He had sent them to escort a herd of horses to the Governor, his nephew, in Monterey, via the Sacramento River route!

The soldiers had camped for the night in the hills of southeastern Napa. In the morning, while they were having breakfast, a troop of mounted Bear Flaggers charged into the camp, with their guns out and ready.

They told the young lieutenant to continue on to Monterey and to inform the Governor that *they were taking command of Sonoma,* and oh, by the way, they were taking the herd of horses too! The lieutenant objected, saying that they never would have overcome his men if they had been prepared for the horsemen. The American leader of the horsemen, who was known for his propensity for violence, and for continually smelling of liquor said, *"No problem. We'll ride out and give you a chance to get ready, and then ride back in again."* Faced with that unappealing prospect, the lieutenant withdrew his objection, relinquished the herd and continued on to Monterey with the message.

The Bear Flaggers were due in Sonoma the next day, and they realized that moving the herd would take more time than they had, so they left the horses in the little valley, planning to return for them later. It seems like that didn't work out as planned, because today that remote area came to be called Wild Horse Valley.

But before the Bear Flaggers raised their banner on the plaza, Sonoma served as the northern most Franciscan Mission, Imperial Spanish Military base, and an official city, or pueblo, complete with a court, judge and records. Sonoma was also settled first because while the native tribes of Sonoma were no pushovers, the Wappo tribe of Napa was *terrifying*. The name comes from the Spanish, 'Guapo,' or 'brave,' which morphed into 'Wappo.'

Their fierce resistance survived the Spanish and the Mexicans, and it was finally the United States Cavalry, battle hardened by the Civil War, who moved the surviving women, children and old men to a coastal reservation, or Rancheria. Most of the braves had been killed in the years of conflict.

The wide variety of grapes grown in Sonoma is different from very focused Napa, where half of the vineyards are Cabernet Sauvignon and most of the rest are its blending grapes: Merlot, Cabernet Franc, Malbec and Petite Verdot. The old Italian American families in Northern Napa grow a fair amount of Zinfandel vines, which lack trellises and instead look like small bushes. In the cool, southern Carneros region along the bay, Chardonnay and Pinot Noir vineyards abound, along with a small amount of Syrah and even Gamay.

In Sonoma, the last time I checked, they grew more than *100 different varieties*. This incredible diversity comes from several factors. Sonoma is almost three times as large as Napa with a much wider variety of climates and soil types that can support a wider selection of wine grapes. Also, the Italian winemaking tradition makes wines for every palate. When they came to America, they saw no reason to change.

While Napa has a mix of American, French, German and Italian winemaking traditions, Sonoma was dominated by immigrant northern Italian families, because the region is similar to *foggy* Piedmonte. Finally, Sonoma is populated in part by the artists and hippies from San Francisco who made their money and moved north. They are innovative and creative and willing to take risks by making wines from 'out of the box' grapes.

In Sonoma, *quality of life* has always mattered more than prestige, whereas Napa is the reverse. People move to Napa because they want to be noticed for their work and success. A large part of Sonoma is called the Redwood Empire with its heavily forested hills. Because it's closer to the ocean, it's green and wet so in many parts of the county you could build a large estate and once the moving trucks leave, your privacy is assured. Even during the time of the native people, Sonoma has been more eclectic and tribal, with fifty or sixty small villages, each having their own language. In Napa, the fierce but insular Wappo tribe dominated the northern valley, while the larger, more social Patwin tribe, whose territory extended over the eastern hills, harvested fish and seafood in the south along the bay.

Those trends are still true. Napa is divided between the upper valley growers and the down valley businesspeople. Sonoma is made up of numerous eclectic communities spread around a big county with very different priorities. You can spot kids who grew up in Napa because they're very motivated for success. The kids from Sonoma are smart and creative, but value privacy. That may be a little oversimplified, but it's mostly true!

Napa growers focus on Cabernet Sauvignon because they can, thanks to the valley's unique terroir, a French word that describes the mix of climate, location, geology and soil vitality. The Cab vines produce more high-quality fruit on less land than most other varietals, and the grapes command the best prices from the wineries. While their thick skins are resistant to bugs and rain, that toughness means they need very bright sunlight, warm days and a long growing season to ripen completely.

They also need cool nights to shut down their metabolism, so the fruit maintains its acid levels and rich flavors.

These conditions are found in great wine regions globally, and Napa's weather produces it consistently. It has made these vineyards California's *most expensive*, on par with the best of France and Italy. Is it any surprise that locally they have a saying, 'Cabernet is King?' But if that is true then Merlot is Queen, because that juicy likable grape shows up in so many blends.

There is another, very obstructive reason the two counties are not traditionally competitive with each other. That's the big line of mountains that rise up between the two counties. They are called the Mayacamas which in the native tongue means '*many springs.*' That remarkable geological feature is part of the secret success of this region. Wine grapes like it dry and this region can go for six months without significant rain, which coincides with the vine's growing cycle. But between the underground springs and overnight fog the vines get the water they need in a form that doesn't promote the biggest threat to grapes, mold and fungus.

The Mayacamas have been a practical obstruction since the days of horse drawn wagons. Family grape growers and winery owners by necessity form long term relationships, often intermarrying. So, for many years the winemakers only tended to buy grapes from the easier to reach vineyards to the north and south before they looked for fruit across the mountains.

Sonoma buys from Mendocino County which sits to the north, known for grapes and cannabis, and Marin

County to the south with their cool weather grapes and great shopping. It is also the way to San Francisco over the Golden Gate Bridge. Napa buys from Lake County, a big growing area to the north and Solano County to the east and south, which provides less expensive grapes and a route to San Francisco over the Bay Bridge.

A story that perfectly describes this dilemma goes back to the early 1970's when Mike Grgich needed chardonnay grapes for Chateau Montelena in Northern Napa. He went to Northern Sonoma to the Bacigalupi family vineyards to get the quality he wanted. The only truck that Charles and Helen Bacigalupi had was a very *underpowered* VW, a version of the iconic van with a truck back. The mountains that separate the vineyards and the winery are high and steep. Helen had to get a running start to make it over the crest, hoping the whole time that no one slower got in her way, because she would lose her precious momentum.

Thanks to bigger, more muscular trucks it's common for Napa and Sonoma wineries to purchase grapes from each other, especially Pinot Noir from the Russian River, and less often Cabernet from Napa, because Cab is so expensive. Like I said, Napa adores his older sister, but in response sometimes Sonoma *just rolls her eyes!*

Chapter Ten
The Power of River Towns

The first thing you need to understand about Napa is that it's a River Town, because everything starts there. In our modern world when we travel by car, train and plane, much faster than any ship, it's easy to forget how important rivers and waterways have been in the development of societies, cultures and markets. Even today, transporting goods by ship is dramatically more efficient compared to every other method. Americans think of our country as special and, in many ways, it is.

American exceptionalism started centuries ago when talented ancestors, braving the odds, went down to the docks and climbed on ships to cross an ocean. Most people feel safer when the floor beneath their feet doesn't move. For my grandmother, Mary Rosamilia, who arrived in New Jersy from Avellino Italy in 1901, it was the *first time she had seen a ship,* and the last time she was on one. The demands of an ocean journey filter out the timid, explaining a great deal about the American personality. We prize courage and audacity!

An equally important and related part of what contributes to America's good fortune is being located on a continent with an abundance of navigable rivers, crossing fertile farmlands. This makes it easy and reasonable to get products to market. This *network* of harbors, protected bays, navigable rivers, great lakes and canals is so widespread in the United States that most people don't realize how rare that is in the rest of the world.

The African Continent and China both have just one navigable river leading to a port. Mexico also has only one navigable river and port. The United States has more great ports fed by navigable river systems than most of the world has put together. Of course, having oceans on each side makes getting here harder, but at least once you arrive there are plenty of choices of good harbors to dock your ship.

The economic power that Northern Europe has wielded for so long comes from a *similar network* of rivers crossing through fertile lands. But those same rivers were also the source of almost endless squabbles over territory because the rivers made it difficult to protect their borders. Germany is the perfect example. They have two wonderful rivers running through their country, but it made them accessible to the armies of their neighbors, so they suffered numerous invasions. The result was that the German people became tremendously unified and organized in order to protect their sovereignty.

In contrast, the USA is *buffered* from the world by two oceans and blessed with friendly neighbors to the north and south. The Mississippi and Missouri Rivers travel from the heartland to the Gulf and both coasts have numerous great bays. New York City sits at the outlet of the great Hudson River and Philadelphia on the banks of the mighty Delaware. These two economic centers are connected by the East Coast's *intercoastal waterway*, a combination of natural and constructed passages stretching three thousand miles from Massachusetts to Texas.

It allows ships to move cargo long distances safely without having to always brave the open sea. Through incredible industry, canals have connected rivers to the Great Lakes, which themselves are a major navigation resource. Where I grew up in New Jersey, which has a remarkable industrial history, there are old *canals* from the early 1800's crisscrossing the state, connecting the rivers together with the farms and manufacturing centers.

Napa is the extreme version of that combination of those two factors: distance and accessibility. No matter which of the traditional population centers you started from, whether by land or sea, reaching Napa required a long, arduous journey and a significant amount of bravery, or foolishness. From a European point of view, Napa was the *'ends of the Earth,'* originally requiring a journey by ship around the tip of south America. Later a traveler could also choose to take the shorter route that required crossing the malarial jungle of Panama, with its torrential rain and cloying humidity on foot. The Spanish called the path that they established to connect the Atlantic to the Pacific 'El Camino Real, the Royal Road', a name they would give to the path that connected the twenty-one Franciscan Missions in California. At the time when the Canal was being constructed, there were still sections of the ancient trail visible alongside the railroad that was built to support that grand construction project.

The opening of the Panama Canal in 1914 was a *monumental* event for the Bay Area. It was celebrated the next year in San Francisco with the Panama Pacific International Exposition, a world's fair that covered a square mile of what is today the city's Marina District. It included contributions from twenty-four countries, and it dramatically showed the world that *'Frisco'* had recovered from the devastating 1906 Earthquake and fires.

The city of Napa sits at the junction of a tremendously fertile valley, and the farthest northern deep-water spot on a navigable river that empties into the San Francisco Bay. From there, ships could reach the entire Bay Area or go through the Golden Gate Pass to the Pacific Ocean and the world beyond. Only a truly adventurous seafarer would find their way up this winding river into this beautiful valley. That is why many of the earliest investors in the valley were *sea captains*. That fact set a theme for attracting brave people, with a worldly view, willing to take a chance.

When you walk up Main Street from First Street, painted on a wall is one of the wonderful murals that talk about the history of Napa. This one, just a block from the river, celebrates the docks, ships and businesses that served this area. But there are many reminders of Napa's seagoing past in the layout of the town and the buildings left behind. *Division Street,* only three and half blocks long, unaligned with the surrounding city's streets, owes its odd angle to its history as a way station where wagons lined up waiting to deliver their products to the river boats.

When you walk around the tree lined streets of 'Old Town' you'll see numerous homes sporting charming railings, banisters and decorative ship's wheels. These are all reminders of the sailing ships that brought those 'old salts' to their final port in Napa. You can always spot the oldest homes because their 'first floor' sat high above the ground to protect the living spaces from the *floods* that often occurred.

On both sides of the river are imposing stone buildings that once served the commercial docks. On the west bank is the Hatt Building that has passed through the hands of several families, and today is the home of the Napa River Inn, several stores, and charming restaurants that enjoy views of the river. If you wait long enough, you'll hear the whistle of the Napa Wine Train as it leaves its rail yard on the far bank.

In the mid 1800's San Franciscans could take a ferry to the city of Vallejo, south of Napa. There they could board the train that would take them north to downtown

Napa, or all the way up the valley to the healing waters of Calistoga.

Just a few steps farther south from the site of the old docks, was a multi-story house of ill repute, which survived from the early shipping days, up until the end of the Second World War. Seventeen miles down the Napa River in Vallejo is Mare Island. This was the Navy's first West Coast base started in 1854. During the war it was one of the busiest shipyards on the planet. On the weekends the base had a ferry boat that would bring sailors to downtown Napa, probably because it was the site of the good bars and fancy ladies.

Also, Downtown Vallejo's bars were swamped with construction workers. Today, eighty years later downtown Napa is quite different. Instead of multiple bars, it's home to the *world's greatest density* of winery tasting rooms. In place of hordes of young sailors, it attracts couples looking to spend a romantic day in wine country.

The current transformation of Downtown Napa's personality has been due entirely to its relationship with the river. The city had always been prone to flooding. When the winter rains came, the Napa River and the Napa Creek would regularly burst their banks and spread out through the downtown. Between the city's founding in the 1840's and 2005 there were *catastrophic* floods over twenty times. We're not just talking about heavy rains that saw water in the streets overshooting the curbs, for which the shopkeepers always had sandbags ready. These major floods would reach the bottoms of the Stop

Signs and take days to recede. It's not surprising that the big hotel chains and restaurants wouldn't invest there. But after a dramatic flood in 2005, the city leaders convinced the Army Core of Engineers, who are responsible for waterways, to begin a decade and a half long transformation of the river. *The river doesn't flood downtown Napa anymore* and soon after work began, major hotels and new restaurants began planning for their arrival.

As they established themselves, winery owners realized that lots of their potential customers were walking those now dry streets. They looked at the numbers and realized that having a downtown tasting room was more reasonable, and profitable, than creating one at their winery. Even larger wineries, with hospitality centers in the valley, have opened tasting rooms near the restaurants and hotels.

Meanwhile in the valley, most of the wineries now require appointments and their tasting fees have dramatically increased. So, downtown Napa has become the favorite alternative for Bay Area folks wanting to come to wine country for the day. They can stroll the sunny streets, visit the many shops, enjoy a tasting, or two, then have some lunch before they head back to the cool fog of San Francisco. That all happened when they negotiated a truce with the river!

Chapter Eleven
The Naming of Mount Saint Helena

One of my favorite stories, because it's both adventurous and romantic, is how Mount Saint Helena got her name. This very pretty mountain towers over the northern end of the Napa Valley, standing just under five thousand feet tall, and looking like *the volcanic cone that she was three million years ago.* Many new visitors to the West Coast, when they first hear the name, confuse this with Mount Saint Helens, the volcano in Washington State that famously erupted in 1980. People are horrible at geography! Saint Helena, in comparison, is about three thousand feet smaller. She's more of a 'designer mountain,' good looking, graceful and accessible.

She does have warm feet, because thermal tubes from more recent volcanos to the north pass under her skirts. Those tubes provide the heat for the popular hot springs that boil to the surface in the town of Calistoga. Sam Brannan, who founded the town in the mid-1800's, claimed it would be the "Saratoga Springs of California." Sam inadvertently named the town when, during a brandy-soaked event for his investors at his hot springs spa, his inebriated tongue claimed it would be "The Calistoga of Sarafornia!" Of course, in a town with such a good sense of humor, there is a *Café Sarafornia.*

While Mount Saint Helena looks like a volcanic cone from the Napa Valley floor, when you see her from Northern Sonoma, sailing over the ridges of the Mayacamas mountain range that separates the two counties, she appears as a rambling series of descending mounds *in the shape of a woman's body.* That distinctive shape is part of one of the stories behind the naming of the mountain. This is the quintessential example of a wine country story because there are at least four versions that all sound mostly feasible. Which story you hear depends on where you are and who is telling it, and how much wine has been consumed.

Not surprisingly, you'll hear different versions of the story in Napa and Sonoma. In Napa, the story goes that the mountain was named by a Russian Princess who climbed the mountain in the 1800's. Many people don't realize that while Northern California was the northern tip of the Spanish empire, it was also the southern tip of the Russian Empire's reach in the Americas. The icy

Russian seal hunting camps in Alaska needed provisions and they saw the temperate Sonoma coast as the solution. Princess Elena, her husband and three children were in the party that traveled in two ships to Sonoma where they established a farming community. Compared to frozen Alaska, this slice of the coast was a little piece of heaven, where the fields for grazing livestock stayed green most of the year, and everything they planted quickly sprouted and prospered.

The locals called it Fort Ross, or 'Rooss,' or 'Rossiya', for Mother Russia. Considering *the diverse languages spoken in the area; Spanish, English, Russian, Polish, Chinese, Kodiak, Pomo, Patwin and Onasai,* it's amazing that the name stayed that close to the original. While that explains how the Russian River Valley got its name, it still seems strange that a Princess would find herself on the far ends of the Earth and have the opportunity to name a mountain.

The story I heard was that the Princess Elena Pavlovna Gagarina, *the niece of the Czarina and an exceptionally beautiful young woman, fell in love with a handsome Count.* He was brave, resourceful and a renowned poet. But Alexander Rotchev's rank was many steps below that of his beloved Elena. In the Russian Court rank mattered, so not surprisingly, the Czarina did not give her blessing for the marriage. Elena followed her heart and they married anyway. Amazingly, the Count's opportunities dried up. After a long wait, he was offered a posting at the camp in Alaska, the farthest and coldest reaches of the Russian Empire. Here's an important lesson, when someone holds your fate in their hands, don't piss off the Czarina! So, the Count bundled his wife and their young children, off to the ends of the Earth.

Fortunately for the young couple, the governor of Alaska saw Alexander as a man he could trust to accomplish a difficult venture. He also probably felt sorry for this sophisticated, young family struggling in the frozen wasteland. So, he assigned Alexander to take those two ships, and his family, and sail south along the coast to establish a farming community.

It had to be done carefully because the British had claimed the coast of Canada. Further south, New England sea captains held sway over what is today Washington and Oregon and dominated shipping along the Pacific Coast. They originally ventured there to hunt whales, but then found a profitable living transporting finished products from the New England workshops and factories to the settlers and gold miners.

On Spain Street in downtown Sonoma is a pretty, Victorian house that is home to a restaurant called the General's Daughter. It was built in New England and transported in pieces in the belly of a sailing ship for General Vallejo as a wedding gift for one of his daughters. His own house, built in the same New England workshops, is a short walk away. It sits below the 'Lachryma Montis' springs, the 'tears of the mountain.' That was also the name of Vallejo's wine brand when he was one of the biggest producers in the North Bay.

The Russians couldn't travel far south without upsetting the Spanish Governor, who resided in

Monterey, and who had a small garrison on the San Francisco Bay. The Spanish considered 'Alta California', as it was known, a wild place. Their settlements there probably only developed due to the spice trade. The Galleons, returning from the Philippines rode the circular Pacific currents. Their first landfall was normally along the Northern California coast. As they made their way south at about six knots, they explored the coast looking for bays where they could moor and take on fresh water and provisions. One of the first bays they discovered was Carmel and that became the home of the first Northern California Franciscan Mission.

So as Alexander and Elena sailed south, they had to find a spot that the English, Americans and Spaniards were not interested in. They settled on a piece of the California coast just north of the Russian River delta. While the river is too shallow for a ship, it was perfect for the sturdy Aleut hunters and their kayaks, which they brought along on their incessant search for furs. To say this spot, covered with towering redwood forests, was remote is an understatement. It was the middle of nowhere! Even today, with good roads and driving in a car it's a hike!

Because Northern California was so difficult to reach, it was a land of brave and capable adventurers, and its fair share of fools. Imagine the splash it created to have this brilliant and sophisticated couple arrive in their midst. That Elena was a true blonde beauty, certainly turned many heads in this land that was populated by dark haired Spaniards and native tribes. Despite the Fort's remote location, the Princess and the Count hosted local dignitaries including General Vallejo and his ally, Chief Solano.

They in turn were welcomed at the General's home in Sonoma. The fact that Mariano Guadalupe Vallejo had been sent north to keep the Russians from expanding their operations to the south seems to have been temporarily forgotten. That is not surprising. *This charming couple, who were so obviously in love,* brought some very appreciated glamour and sophistication to this rustic place. From Mariano's point of view, they were a wonderful addition, and Mexico City was very far away.

Princess Elena and her husband Alexander were the last directors of Russia's settlement in California. Well before the Czar's final days, seventy years later, they abandoned it because of increasing pressure from the Americans who were flooding the area. Here we get to the first two stories about the naming of Mount Saint Helena. Before they left, Elena, or 'Helena' took the opportunity to travel throughout the area with two Russian scientists who were recording their observations of the area. Of course, they brought along some hardy helpers with rifles because this area had a lively community of fierce braves and California Grizzly Bears.

From Sonoma they could see Mount Mayacamas, as the natives called Mount Saint Helena, towering over the mountain ridge to the east. Elena, with the scientists and bodyguards, trekked over the hills and climbed the almost 5,000-foot peak. She was clearly a very vigorous woman because it's quite a climb. The name was changed from Mayacamas, which meant 'many springs,' when the climbing party installed a bronze plaque at the peak declaring it to be Mount Saint Helena and including the names of various Russian dignitaries.

The name Elena is a variation of Helena, Ilona and Helen. In Napa, the story goes that it was named for Princess Elena. The second variation was that Princess Elena named it for the Czarina's patron Saint, 'Helena,' the mother of the Roman Emperor Constantine, who was the Pontifex Maximus of the Roman Church and coincidentally a famous Astrologer. It was Mama Helena who convinced her son to make Christianity the Empire's official religion. *As the mother of Russia, it was natural that Czarina Alexandra's patron Saint* would be the Emperor's mother who changed the Christian world.

One could imagine that Princess Elena, a sophisticated young woman *banished to the far reaches of the Earth,* wanted to get back in the Czarina's good graces, and return to the comforts of the royal court. We can also imagine her writing the Czarina a letter in her beautiful Cyrillic hand, "Dear Auntie Alexandra, I've named a beautiful mountain for your favorite Saint, can I come home now, please?" and then sealing the letter with wax, a prayer and a tear.

It was not long after the naming of the mountain that the Russians gave up their 'Fort' on the Sonoma coast. Did she and her husband return home to the Russian Court, or did they make their way in California? No one seems to know. Hopefully, their future was as interesting as their past.

There is a second, more romantic version of this story. In that one, Count Alexander and a party of scientists climbed the mountain and installed the plaque. The Helena he was thinking about was his beloved wife Elena, the mother of his children, who had followed him to the ends of the Earth for love.

Now, if you are in Sonoma, the naming of Mount Saint Helena is a different tale. When you see the mountain from the Santa Rosa plains, it's even more impressive than the solitary cone you see from southern Napa. In Sonoma it becomes a long, rambling mountain ridge. In an area where the hills stand between 1,000 and 2,000 feet, Mount Saint Helena, at just under 5000 feet can be seen for many miles around. I heard this story of the naming of Mount Saint Helena from an archaeologist at Fort Ross, so I would normally give it a bit more credence than I give to other wine country stories I've heard.

That's because the stories you hear in Wine Country often benefit from artistic additions, inspired by both the storyteller and the audience being under the influence of some wonderful wines. Our stories are a perfect example of that! With that said, there are some other factors that cast some doubt on this source for the name.

According to my friend at Fort Ross, the mountain was already called Mount Saint Helena before Elena, or Alexander climbed the mountain with their plaque. In this story, the Mountain was first named by the Franciscan missionary, Altamira, who saw it from, what is today, Santa Rosa, which has the distinction of being the Northern most major California city with a Spanish name.

Naming every place after Saints, or Angels was normal. Santa Rosa gets its name from 'Saint Rose of Lima,' the first Saint of the Americas.

The story goes that the shape of Saint Helena, which resembles a reclining woman, reminded Altamira of a funerary statue in a church in France. The Patron Saint of the church was Saint Helena. While being named by one of the Franciscan missionaries is always historically notable, this particular Franciscan's history in Northern California is so checkered and vainglorious that it makes you wonder, whether his story about naming the mountain was true.

We know that he established the Sonoma Mission at Los Carneros, close to the bay, *because he was very wary of the tribes to the north* that he would encounter on the way to Santa Rosa.

While the Governor in Monterey had given him soldiers to help, it was a small contingent and Altamira was famously unpopular with the local tribes. In any case, what are the chances that he traveled up the Sonoma Valley to where he could see the mountain? It is more likely that he received descriptions of the mountain from soldiers and recorded the name on a map! *But did he name it, or was he told the name and wove a good story to give himself the credit?*

Cartography is an interesting profession. Here is an interesting fact that is possibly not taught in schools anymore. The way the Americas got their name was because one of the first popular maps of the Americas was based on charts provided by Amerigo Vespucci.

He signed his name very prominently on the unexplored landmass beyond the coastline, so the mapmakers assumed that was its name. Later when they realized their mistake they changed it on later maps, depending on which countries claimed the various parts of the coast, but the name stuck. Amerigo does have the distinction of being the first person to postulate that this was an entirely different continent, and not part of Asia, as had been previously assumed.

The adventures of the Franciscan Missionaries north of the bay were short-lived. Eight years after the Sonoma Mission was established under Imperial Mexico, the Mexican Revolution happened and the leaders in Mexico City considered the church an agent of the aristocracy. Any native-born Spaniards, who had not become citizens of Mexico, were forced out and Padre Altamira was sent packing back to Barcelona and was never heard from again. The missions were secularized and the mission buildings on the Sonoma Plaza became General Vallejo's property.

Like so many Sonoma buildings on the Plaza, the San Francisco Solano Mission survived because they could not afford to replace it. Its sister Mission to the south in San Rafael was taken down when they built a very impressive Spanish style church. Years later, when a group wanted to build a re-creation of the mission building, they had no record of what it looked like. So, they built it using an image found on a popular set of postcards. One slight problem! The publishing company didn't know what the building looked like either.

So, they substituted a different view of the very pretty Carmel mission, which had survived nicely.

One More Story

Now those are the first three stories about the naming of Mount Saint Helena, and I promised you four. While you can see Saint Helena from Sonoma, she is very much Napa's Mountain. The town of Napa was founded at the northernmost point that can be reached with a sailing ship so many of Napa's earliest investors were sea captains. The Mexicans didn't prefer Napa for two reasons. First, it's much drier than Sonoma, and second, it was inhabited by the fierce Onasai/Wappo tribe and a multitude of giant California Grizzly bears. *It was much safer to stay in Sonoma!*

But many of the Americans who settled in Napa were sailors, soldiers, military men, mountain men and wagon train leaders. They were adventurous and accustomed to dealing with trouble.

To provide a little context, let's mention that when California became part of the United States, the Presidio at Sonoma became the central Fort for Northern California. Many of the famous Civil War Generals visited the area and the famous General Hooker, whose exploits are well recorded, lived in Sonoma for many years. Today there is a nearby creek named for him and his home, which is just off the Sonoma Plaza, serves as the local Historical Society. There is an old story that the term "Hooker" comes from the numerous 'loose women' that frequented his headquarters. Ever since his service in the Mexican American war there were always ladies around who admired the 'Handsome General." *As the Army moved from camp to camp, they became known as Hooker's Girls.* While the term hooker did appear in print in the years before the General came to prominence, his tendency to run a camp that other officers described as part bar and part brothel, surely helped to make the term more popular.

But back to the story! In Napa, it was the ship captains who left their mark, and their homes, alongside the river. With many of them being New Englanders, they favored Victorian-style homes, but with a California flair. As word of Napa's beautiful, fertile valley and easy access to the bay spread among the sea going community, it attracted more sailors. One of them was *a sea captain from England. He arrived with a purse full of money after a successful trip* and went looking for land in Napa. An adventurous soul looking for a good deal, the captain looked in the far north end of the valley, finally buying a large piece of land that included Mount Saint Helena.

As he stood atop this grand mountain and looked out over the beautiful valley, he realized it was his mountain to name. So, he named it after the ship that had brought him to San Francisco and provided the wealth he needed to make a home in this American Eden. The name of that ship was the 'Saint Helena.' Was it just a coincidence? Did he arrive and find that the mountain had the same name as his ship? Sailors are a superstitious lot, and he could have taken that as a lucky sign! Of course, with time and enough good bottles of wine and brandy, the story more than likely evolved until it was the Captain that coined the name for his pretty little mountain, sitting at the top of a gorgeous valley, north of the San Francisco Bay.

I am not sure which of these stories is true, although *I expect that there's some truth here and there, in bits and pieces.* The one thing that I do know is true and obvious, Mount Saint Helena knew what she wanted to be called.

The Silverado Trail

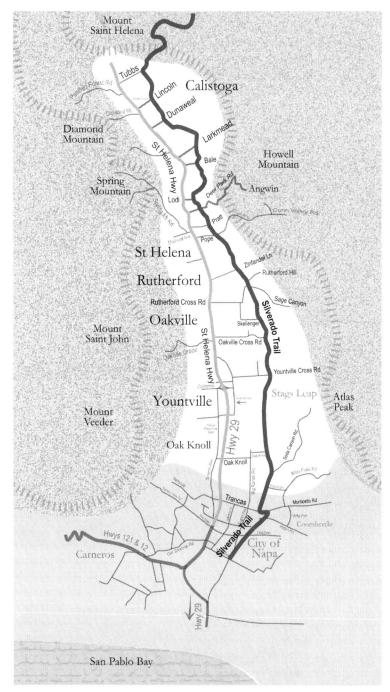

Silverado Vineyards

Chapter Twelve
The Romance of the Silverado Trail

The Silverado Trail is the quintessential California road that travels along the eastern side of the Napa Valley at the foot of the Vaca Mountains. It started as a native trail that wound its way through the hills to get above the winter flooding on the valley floor. It was made into a road by western settlers in the 1860s, to provide a winter alternative when the main road that goes up the center of the valley, Saint Helena Highway, *washed* out in the seasonal rains. But for centuries before that, the trail served a key role in the tribal economies.

Traces of the original native trail can still be found at the top of the valley within sight of Mount Saint Helena. From there it would have been a two day walk south to where the Napa River and the Napa Creek merge.

Yes, they are both named 'Napa,' and they meet right where the city of Napa was founded in 1850. south of there the river gets dramatically deeper and straighter. The Onasai, who the Spanish called the Wappo for fierce, lived in the upper valley. In the south were the Patwin, whose lands stretched along the edge of the bay and across the southern hills to the east. The Onasai would *make a deal* with the Patwin to use their 'sákas' or reed boats. From there the Onasai would have an easy, three-hour paddle south to the Sacramento River.

At that junction, just before the joined rivers empty into the great bay, there was a tribe called the 'Carquinez' whose name meant the traders. Today the bridge that spans those narrows is named for them. From there the Onasai could travel to the east on the Sacramento, or west into the bay and the world beyond. What did the Onasai have to trade? Power and efficiency, in the form of razor-sharp obsidian weapons and tools!

The Napa Valley was only shared by two human tribes, and *a formidable tribe of grizzly bears.* The upper valley, as far south as modern Yountville, was controlled by the very insular 'Onosai,' meaning the 'Outspoken Ones.' They had spread south from the lake region in order to gain control of the black volcanic glass deposits at the northeastern part of the trail. Today, that area is called Glass Mountain.

This 'glass' is actually volcanic obsidian formed millions of years ago when silica rich lava ejected from Mount Saint Helena plunged into cold lakes, instantly fusing and producing a fractured glass that is both strong and incredibly sharp. The Onosai depended on the trail and the river to trade knives, arrowheads, hatchets, and scraping tools that they fashioned from the obsidian chips.

Remnants of their handiwork have been found as far south as modern Los Angeles and as far east as Utah. The local tribes called that vital convergence of the waters where they could easily launch their boats the 'fairy village.' It seems a strange name, until you realize that ancient traditions teach that spirits and ghosts prefer to reside close to running water. This was the northern edge of the area controlled by the more populous Patwin tribe, whose villages spread all the way east into today's Solano County. Because that junction of river and creek flooded so dependably, no tribe would make a permanent encampment there, but it made a wonderful place to trade and launch their sákas.

When the Americans came, this was the location where they could sail their ships, so they built docks and warehouses there, and eventually a sprawling town. The fertility and abundance of the valley attracted sailing ships, bringing supplies and looking for local products to trade in distant markets. Many of Napa Valley's most historic wineries were built in the 1800's by wealthy ship Captains.

There are two stories behind the trail's distinctive name. The first starts with the *gold rush* in the Sierra Madre Mountains, a five-day wagon ride to the east. It attracted so many hopeful prospectors from around the world, that sailing ships arriving in San Francisco's harbor were often *stranded* there, when the crews abandoned them and headed for the hills. But refining gold requires mercury to capture the grains that are mixed with the sand. So, when that liquid metal was discovered around the hot springs that are found throughout the Napa Valley, that provided a new opportunity for the miners, and they needed a way to get there.

'Helena' as she is known locally, is just under five thousand feet tall. She's a pretty mountain with an elegant volcanic cone, that sees a frosting of snow every five years or so. When she erupted three million years ago, along with a string of other smaller mountains in Napa and Sonoma, they shaped this area's distinctive look and geology. The mercury miners, who were a particularly 'loony lot' due to their exposure to that metallic neurotoxin, named the trail after mercury's traditional title, *quicksilver*.

So, today's Silverado Trail was originally named for the Roman God, Mercury, the patron of healers and writers. Not so many years later, silver was discovered on Mount Saint Helena and the name 'Silverado Trail' remained perfectly appropriate and helpful to miners looking for work. When you stand on the slopes of the Mayacamas Mountains opposite Mount Saint Helena you can still spot the old mine's tailings, those mounded piles left behind on the graceful slopes.

As the traffic up valley increased, the locals improved the trail. Gradually its path moved to the west, closer to the edge of the valley floor. There are still parts that overlay the original, single person wide path, where countless pairs of feet carried food, supplies and obsidian tools to trade. In the upper part of the valley, you can see spots where the *steel lined wagon wheels wore grooves into the volcanic rock* that makes up those hillsides.

Today the 'Trail' is not as well-known as Saint Helena Highway, called Highway 29 by the locals. That road travels along the wide, flat valley floor, with its rich, deep soil. The Silverado Trail instead skirts the rocky, steep benchlands formed by the volcanic ridges that line the eastern edge of the valley. When the railroad tracks were laid to bring tourists to Calistoga's healing hot springs, they were run alongside Saint Helena Highway. So, while the 'Trail' was locally helpful, it wasn't widely known, until some small fame came to it thanks to a Scottish author.

Robert Louis Stevenson was *very much in love with* Fanny Van de Grift, an American magazine writer he met in Europe. Although there was a spark, she resisted his proposal for marriage, due to his malnourished, pale appearance, love of drink, uncertain income, and the fact that she was already married, with a child. She left him and England's wet climate behind and booked passage on a sailing ship home to New York, and then across the continent to her home in California. Fanny arrived safely but sickly from the arduous journey.

Robert, however, was a poet in love, so he followed her. He arrived in San Francisco in an equally pitiful state, with no guarantee that Fanny had not reconciled with her husband, or found a new handsome, healthy golden haired, California lover. Fortunately for

RLS, Fanny had not replaced him in her heart, and she opened her loving arms to his renewed marriage proposal. Why wouldn't she? Louis, as he was known among his friends, had left everything behind, crossed oceans and traveled halfway around the world to find her, he was obviously committed, and very much in love!

They had to wait for her divorce to be finalized in order to marry and then they spent the first few nights of their wedded bliss in San Francisco's famous *Palace Hotel*. Their friends, taking into consideration the newlyweds' sickly appearance, suggested that they honeymoon at the *healing spas* of Napa. The hot springs had become famous for their ability to restore health, along with the beautiful scenery, bountiful fresh food and 'good air.'

They stayed at a hotel in Saint Helena and found the climate kind, the air and food wonderful and the sunlight luminous. So, they searched for a way to extend their stay that would not use up their limited funds.

One of the locals pointed the young couple towards an abandoned mining camp on the flanks of Mount Saint Helena, where they found a two-story cabin that they *squatted* in for a two-month long honeymoon. As they gradually regained their vitality in this new Eden, Robert and Fanny were impressed so much by Napa that not surprisingly, the location found its way into his writings.

In his most famous book, 'Treasure Island,' the location of 'Lookout Mountain' was based on Mount Saint Helena, where they made their first home together, and there was more! During their sojourn they traveled throughout the valley, including visits to the Petrified Forest on top of the Mayacamas Mountains and the nearby Schramsberg Winery. They were thoroughly impressed by the wineries wonderful location, the beautiful buildings, the barrel caves dug by Chinese miners and their generous host's excellent wines.

Robert and Fanny must have been amazed by the Schram's success. Here was Jacob, a German immigrant barber, married to Annie, a local German American girl, who together made a farmstead out of a heavily wooded, up valley hillside that they turned into their own paradise.

The Stevensons' story was contained in a travelog that Robert wrote called the *'Silverado Squatters'* about their home on the mountain. It contains the often-quoted phrase, for which Napa marketing folks have been eternally grateful, *"Wine is bottled poetry."*

But how did these young folks, with limited money, get around the valley in the 1880's? At that time, people either walked, rented horses or a wagon. They might also rely on the flexibility and generosity of the local stagecoach drivers, colorful characters, who traveled along both the Saint Helena Highway and the Silverado Trail!

Luckily, they were befriended by a man called 'John Silverado' because he ran the Silverado Trail stagecoach line. He was a very tall, commanding gent who towered over most other folks, earning him the popular moniker 'Long John.' As any reader of the great adventure novel 'Treasure Island' knows, the swashbuckling, peg-legged pirate at the heart of that story is named Long John Silver! I have often wondered if that flamboyant wagon driver, a predecessor of the local tour guides, who are themselves a colorful group, happened to wear a patch over one eye? Argh!

Above: Stage Coach Driver, Shotgun and Passengers
Opposite: Stag's Leap Wine Cellars

Chapter Thirteen
Judging California in Far Off Paris

As tour guides tell it, the Judgment of Paris is a simple story. In June of 1976, a competition was held in Paris pitting the top California wines against the top French wines. The Californians, most notably, the 'Napans,' routed the *'Frenchies'* and put our little Valley on the world-wide wine map. Pretty simple, yes?

But of course, in Wine Country, there's always more to the story and the genuinely interesting pieces are stuck in various memories all over both counties. The story has been told countless times by tour guides and winery hosts. It was even made into a small budget, but popular movie that was shot on location called 'Bottle Shock.' It was seen by a surprisingly large number of people thanks to the airlines featuring it on California bound flights. I've heard all kinds of inside stories about both the 'Judgment' and the movie, thanks to being both a local guide and television producer. At the wine and travel writer's conference at Saint Helena's Meadowood Resort, I spent quite a bit of time with the original screenwriter, Ross Schwartz, hearing about how the story turned into a movie.

Ross is an entertainment attorney in Los Angeles, and his father was a prominent television producer whose credits included Gilligan's Island. It seems to me that if you live in Los Angeles and you have connections to the industry, you must write a movie script. Well, Ross wanted to try his hand at writing one, so his wife told him about this wacky story she heard about the American wines beating the French wines back in 1976. When Ross looked into it, he realized that the owner of Chateau Montelena, Jim Barrett, was, like Ross, an attorney.

Jim had given up his San Francisco law practice to pursue his dream of producing a great wine at the top of the Napa Valley. Even better for the sake of the story, previous to their win, the winery was on the ropes. Even in that precarious situation, Jim *didn't want his wines included* in the tasting, because in the previous years the French had always taken the highest scores. He didn't want to give this English shop owner and his French wine writers the opportunity to pump up their wines at the expense of the Americans.

But unbeknownst to him, his son Bo snuck some bottles out of the winery and got them on the plane.

When they won top honors, the new fame brought them a surge of business as New York restaurants called wanting to put 'Montelena' on their lists. This was the kind of great underdog story that Americans love. So, Ross writes the script, and one day while delivering a contract to a friendly producer he mentions it, asking if they would like to take a look. The producer said yes, so Ross sent it over.

A little while later they called Ross and said, "It's a great script, but it's *only going to cost three or four million* to produce, and we don't do anything less than fifty. But my production manager is going to call you and explain why we can't do it." Now Ross thought that was a little strange, so he said, "I understand, he doesn't need to call me." But his producer friend said, "It's no problem, you see, my production manager really likes the story, so he's going to call you."

A couple of days later he gets a call from the production manager, who says, "It's too small for us, *but I have friends* who produce the Sonoma Film festival. They know everyone up there that you need to know to get this made, so I sent them the script. If they say yes, they want to do it, we'll arrange the financing." Now Ross thought, this is getting interesting.

A while after meeting Ross, I interviewed the movie's co-producer for our TV show 'Wine Country at Work'. Marc and Brenda Lhormer had been in the Silicon Valley events business until they moved to Sonoma and became co-directors of the already existing Sonoma Film Festival. Marc gave me the next part of the story.

"I got a call from a fella I met through the Film Festival. He told me about the script and suggested that we produce it. I told him that we weren't movie producers, and we didn't know how to do that! He told me that with a movie like this it's about two things. First you find the right people, and second you connect with the people in charge of the locations where you want to film. Well, through the festival we've met plenty of directors, actors and videographers, and we knew all the people in charge of the places in Sonoma where we would need to film. Then he said, 'If you'll produce the movie, we'll find the financing!' How could we say no?"

As they began the project, an unexpected player entered the game. George Taber, the writer who reported the story and authored a book about the 'Judgement', was in talks with a producer. The movie would focus, in big part, on Montelena's Croatian American winemaker, Mike Grgich. Ross's script focused on the relationship between Jim and Bo Barrett, and while Mike was a character, *he was not the star.* So, Mike said he didn't want to be mentioned in their film.

After the 'Judgement' in 1976 Mike cofounded the Grgich Hills Winery on July 4th, 1977. Not surprisingly, with that other production in their rear-view mirror, Marc and Brenda became focused on their film being first to market. While the story was centered on Napa and Paris, the movie was filmed in Sonoma, except for one fun scene at Montelena. It is the only segment where there is a visual reference to Mike Grgich. In it a pretty blonde intern is hosing down a big wood basket press on the crush pad while a group of men sit on the wall watching. One of the smaller actors sported a vest and a *beret* like Mike wore every day. Since the movie needed a winemaker, they included Mike's Mexican American assistant, Gustavo Brambila. After the movie came out Gustavo opened his own tasting room in downtown Napa while Marc and Brenda went on to found the Napa Film Festival.

The story that most guides tell is only quasi true. That's not to say that the American wines didn't resoundingly prove themselves against the French, because they did! The French complained that the wines were too young, and with proper aging they would prevail. So to prove that the tasting wasn't a fluke, various groups have repeated it more than thirty times over the years with the original wines. The Californians have *prevailed* every time, although it hasn't always been the same California wines that came out on top.

The reason for their success is simple. Wines are made in the vineyard. Napa and Sonoma are further south so they get warmer daytime weather than the vineyards of France. Also, their grapes get rain free skies for most of the growing season, which the French vintners could only dream about. Great wine grapes require very bright sunlight to produce rich flavors and deep colors. Napa and Sonoma sit immediately north of the shallow, *reflective* San Pablo Bay, which throws even more sunshine into the valleys.

The unique combination of having coasts along both the bay and the ocean produces the chilly nights that allow the grapes to hold on to their flavors and vital structure. Just off the coast are some of the deepest canyons in the Pacific Ocean, and when that frigid water wells up and encounters the hot sunshine it produces the famous Bay Area fog banks.

These flow up the valley nightly during the driest time of the year and coat the grapevines with cool water, which evaporates quickly in the morning sun. From the point of view of a grapevine, Napa and Sonoma simply have better growing conditions.

The name, 'The Judgment of Paris' implying a competition, first appeared as the title of an article in the revered New York Times. It was a *misnomer*, because the event was an annual wine tasting to celebrate the longtime friendly relationship between the two countries, where the French wines consistently outshone the Americans. It was sponsored by a British wine shop owner, Steven Spurrier who was also a partner in the Academy of Wine in Paris, which was France's first significant school focused on tasting and evaluating wine.

George Taber covered the tasting for the *New York Times* because he liked hanging out at the shop for the free samples. If the idea of a Brit owning a wine shop in Paris seems odd to you, it shouldn't. While the French have centuries of experience making wine, dating back to when the invading Celts and Romans arrived with vines in their wagons, the French didn't typically transport it beyond their shores.

It was the British who were their best customers, and it was the British ships that carried the French bottles to customers throughout Europe and the world. The wine from Madeira, where the British frequently bought wine to sell in India, was magically improved by the long, hot sea journey, rolling around in the belly of British sailing ships. My English clients are always more knowledgeable about the world's wines than either my French or Italian clients. While those two countries are the biggest wine producers, the makers tend to know their own region's well, but don't often look beyond their own backyard.

During the movie shoot we were living in Sonoma, and we watched the production crew turn the downtown around the Plaza into Paris. Meanwhile, our son Julian, who was connected to the theater union, was involved in building the sets. During my years of touring, I've visited all the vineyards where the grapes were grown in both Sonoma and Napa, and the vineyards and wineries where the movie was shot and met numerous people who were involved in the original 'Judgment' and the movie, so I thought I had a pretty good handle on the story.

But then I read a wonderful article by Esther Mobley, of the *San Francisco Chronicle*, where she gave credit to the women who were the unsung heroes of this saga. At the time of the tasting in Paris a young American woman, Patricia Gastaud-Gallagher, was a partner in the Académie du Vin. Patricia was in charge of organizing the annual French American tastings each year. Remember, it was the French that helped a young America throw off the British yoke, so you couldn't expect a Brit to handle that particular wine celebration.

Patricia had previously been hamstrung by the quality of the New York State wines that she could get from her friends at the American Embassy. They had heard that America's best wines were being grown in California, but production was still small, and they were not exporting bottles to Europe.

It was 1976, the year of America's Bi-Centennial and Patricia was a member of the 'Daughters of the American Revolution', a club that traces their families back to colonial times. Not surprisingly, she wanted to make that year's tasting *special*. Where to start? She contacted a California wine writer for suggestions, who put her in touch with a woman tour guide, Joanne Dickenson DePuy, who lived in Northern California. Joanne brought groups of California winemakers to France, so she knew all the important winemakers in Napa and Sonoma.

Luckily for the Californians, the Brits are always up for traveling for the sake of wine, so, a month before the event, Spurrier and his wife Bella visited Napa. Joanne drove them around the valley to her favorite wineries where they tasted the recent vintages and selected bottles for the event. Steven and Bella paid *full price* for the bottles, even though they were offered an industry discount. Of course, the bottles only cost about five or six dollars at the time. Quite a difference compared to what they are going for now. Stephen and Bella headed back to Europe confident their bottles would be shipped.

As the time for the tasting session neared it looked like the bottles would be tied up in customs for who knew how long? Luckily, Joanne, *tour guide extraordinaire,* came to their rescue. She was about to embark on a tour with a group of local winemakers to France. At that time, airline passengers were permitted to carry two bottles of wine in their carryon luggage, so Joanne arranged for her guests to carry Spurrier's bottles. That was a critical decision because the wines were carried by people who knew a thing or two about handling bottles, and they arrived in close to pristine condition. Transportation is not wine's best friend.

As an aside, for many years Americans who drank French wines in America, and especially on the west coast, rarely had a true impression of those vintages unless they tasted them in France. That's because the wines were shipped in unrefrigerated containers where the heat often destroyed the flavors, especially when the ships traversed the tropics on the way through the Panama Canal. It was only when the high-end distributors started springing for the cost for refrigerated containers that the west coast market for French wines exploded.

In the Bay Area, premium wineries won't ship bottles during the hottest weather. I often tell my clients that when they taste wines at the winery, they are at their best. When a bottle of wine is transported over a long distance it can suffer from *bottle shock,* from which the movie took its name. The combination of shaking and temperature changes locks up the aromas and flavors. It's best to wait for a week or so for the wine to recover so that wonderful personality can return! And it does!

So, the wine bottles were hand delivered to Stephen well before tasting. He had tasted the California wines where they were made, and the experience must have convinced him that they could compare well with the French wines. So, *at the last minute*, he did something quite different from previous tastings. He covered the bottles with paper bags, so the tasting wouldn't be colored by the judge's history with the labels.

The tasting begins and the judges, a collection of important French wine writers, taste their way through the many selections, recording their scores as they go. During the tasting they're commenting back and forth, claiming to recognize certain wonderful French vintages and brands. Finally, all the scores were handed in and the paper bags were taken off the bottles. As the scores were tabulated, everyone realized that the French judges had given *the highest scores* to two American wines, the Chateau Montelena Chardonnay, and the Stag's Leap Wine Cellars Cabernet Sauvignon.

It upset one of the critics so much that she grabbed her scores back, and her friend Patricia completely understood why. What she intended as an educational, comparative tasting, to celebrate American French Unity, Spurrier and Taber were spinning as a competition. A few days later Taber's article appeared on the *front page* of the New York Times, the respected and influential town crier for a city that, at that time, consumed much more imported wine than Californian!

Part Two

While the French paid this event little attention, it was a big deal to the Americans. Understanding its significance in the global wine market requires looking at the context. France, like most of Western Europe, has a long tradition of growing grapes and making wine. For centuries wine had been the only safe, potable and storable beverage other than pure well and spring water from the countryside.

In the cities wine was added to water so the alcohol could make it safe. But then ships brought *coffee* from Arabia, *tea* from China and *chocolate* from south America, all drinks that were high in antioxidants and caffeine. More importantly, they were made with boiled water that killed most pathogens. Then the Dutch brought Arabian *distilling technology* from Spain, where it was used to make perfumes and medicines. But in Northern Europe and England, they used it to produce cheap *Gin* from grains and juniper berries.

In England, the combination of that intoxicating drink, so much stronger than beer, ran into the industrial revolution, which dispossessed generations of country craftspeople. This suddenly impoverished class moved to the cities looking for work, where many turned to thievery and Gin to survive. As increasing crime overwhelmed the jails, retired naval ships of the line were moored in London Harbor as prisons. These horrifically housed prisoners became the first unwilling immigrants to the Australia penal colony on the other side of the world, that fortunately, turned out to be a wonderful place to grow wine grapes.

Faced with this new competition from these various drinks for the first time, the winemakers had to *'up their game'* to survive. While the more remote winemakers, like those in Burgundy struggled, the French vintners in Bordeaux, with their ready access to seaports and their British shipping partners, continued to thrive in this new, global market. Many of their most revered wineries date their first great vintages from this period, when they started playing for keeps. So, by 1976, the French winemakers were bringing centuries of experience to Spurrier's wine shop in Paris, making them a sure bet against the newbie Americans.

It seemed *implausible* that the California winemakers could take the top honors, Montelena and Stag's Leap were only recently started and were depending on grapes that other people had planted. What's equally amazing is that Bay Area wineries took multiple spots in the top five for both the red and white wines. The rich wine culture they have today was a California dream for the future, but suddenly that dream seemed much more possible. Remember, at the time this was happening, the California Wine Country looked like the Wild West, with growers wearing *cowboy hats* and driving pickup trucks.

The Californian's did have a couple of ringers. First among them was Russian born, French trained André Tchelistcheff, today called the Godfather of California winemaking. Andre laid out many of the important vineyards in the region and consulted widely with vintners, while directing winemaking at both Beaulieu Vineyards and Buena Vista in Sonoma. His trusted assistant for many years was Mike Grgich. They connected in part because Andre, besides speaking Russian, French and English, also spoke Croatian.

Here is another funny coincidence. Joanne Dickenson DePuy had been trying to unsuccessfully to convince André to lead a tour to France with her. He resisted until his wife convinced him to do it. Dorothy Tchelistcheff was a native Californian, a few years his junior, who ran their business behind the scenes. She knew that the connections they would make during a tour would be good for their consulting business. The three of them were busy herding a group of winemakers around France at the time of the tasting, when news of the results reached them while they were having lunch at a winery in Bordeaux.

Despite the fact that this was shockingly good news, especially since some of the winemakers in the Judgment were in the group, Andre insisted that they not make any fuss to avoid insulting their hosts. But the moment they got back on the bus celebrations *erupted*.

Wine was not the big business in Napa and Sonoma that it is today. There were more *plum* trees than grapevines in Napa and more *apple* trees in Sonoma. But great wines had been produced there before, starting in the late 1800's. As they considered their future, the question in the mind of many North Bay growers was whether or not there was a market for their high-quality wines? During WWII, when the European wineries were out of

America's reach, the more established wineries found a small market for the premium bottles they produced. But once the war ended, the European winemakers broke through the cellar walls where they had hidden their best wines. Pretty soon their labels reappeared on the restaurant wine lists.

That argument about whether the North Bay growers should make premium, or jug wines was the source of the famous feud between the Mondavi brothers. Robert wanted to aim for the stars while Peter wanted to keep their feet firmly on the Earth. That's not surprising considering that Robert was the marketer while Peter was the grower and winemaker.

When Robert left Charles Krug, which was the family business, he started the Robert Mondavi Winery in 1966. *His first winemaker was Warren Winarski, who four years later founded Stag's Leap Wine Cellars.* There Warren crafted the 1973 Cabernet Sauvignon blend that earned the highest red wine score at the 'Judgment.'

You can understand why the California grape growers are risk averse. In the late 1800's and the 1970's the root louse, Phylloxera, decimated their vines. Then in 1919, Prohibition closed all but a handful of wineries. In the following thirteen years bootleggers converted society to hard liquor, stealing their market. Many of them abandoned vineyards, and instead planted fruit and nut trees, or brought in livestock. The rest survived by selling grapes to the home winemakers, and the occasional jug of homemade to their neighbors.

At the time of the 'Judgment', some growers were making small amounts of premium wine, in part to show that they could. Warren's winery was in the Stags Leap district, located in the southeastern corner of the Valley. Until the 'Judgment' it was considered a backwater among the growers. That's because most of the work at that time was done from the seat of a tractor, so the growers preferred vineyards like those in Oakville and Rutherford, where they could drive straight and level for a long way before they had to turn around.

Stags Leap is filled with slopes and cut by canyons. *The small amount of level land near the river quickly rises into the rocky bench lands at the foot of the eastern hills.* It was not considered prime territory, until suddenly one of the local wines was on the front page of the New York Times. Then everybody paid attention!

The same conditions that made the vineyards less attractive for tractor farmed jug wines, makes it perfect for premium grapes, because all those nooks and crannies bounce the sunlight around and capture the evening fog, so it lingers through the morning. As the sunlight streams through the mist, the refracting colors enrich the flavors, adding fruity complexity.

As the hot sun sets on the western facing vineyards, the heat makes the vines pull more sulfur from the soil to deal with the heat. This turns into tannins that help the wine age properly. So, you get the bright fruit at the top and the woody flavors that create a solid foundation underneath. The complexity is surprising and enthralling!

But there's more to the story because an American Chardonnay also scored the highest, in a field filled with spectacular bottles. Chateau Montelena was an unlikely champion for Chardonnay because Calistoga is the *hottest* part of the valley. For generations, the local farmers focused on heat-loving Zinfandel and there are still plenty of those distinctive vineyards to be found there, with their cute, shrub shaped vines. But Chardonnay thrives in a cooler climate, and if you have the money, you can buy grapes. So, Jim Barrett, who, together with partners had revived Montelena 1972, told their winemaker, Mike Grgich, to find some Chardonnay grapes, because Chard was always a good seller.

Mike found the grapes over the mountains on the cool Sonoma benchlands above the Russian River. Even though this is not a great distance from Calistoga as the crow flies, the climate is dramatically different. It gets more of the cool breezes and fogs that roll in from the Pacific Ocean, and it's bisected by the cold Russian River that descends from the northern mountains of Mendocino.

The vineyards are moderately warm and dry during the day, but prone to cool fogs overnight that drench the vines with dew. The mix of extremes makes this a tremendous growing area for all kinds of plants. The famous botanist, Luther Burbank, did much of his work in nearby Santa Rosa, including creating a potato variety to save Ireland from the blight. He said that, of any place he had ever visited, Sonoma County was "the chosen spot of all the earth as far as nature is concerned." And he called the Redwood Empire, the great forests that blanket the Pacific coast, *the place "most blessed by nature."*

Today, the region is home to numerous Pinot Noir and Chardonnay vineyards, but at the time of the Judgment of Paris, it was mostly apple orchards and hops that covered the hills. The vineyards were mostly in the warmer Dry Creek Valley, farmed by Italian American families who grew Zinfandel and Olive trees, because it's truly impossible to live any kind of good life without wine and olive oil, or so I've been told.

The Chardonnay grapes came from the Bacigalupi family vineyards, which sit where the southern edge of the warm Dry Creek Valley meets the northern edge of the cool Russian River Valley. This transitional zone is capable of great complexity and the family has owned their little piece of paradise since 1956. There is a wonderful photo of Mike and Helen Bacigalupi, neither of which are very tall, standing in front of the vines that towered over them.

Mike was famous for being a *hard* bargainer, but Helen was nobody's fool, so I imagine they came to a fair price for those five tons of grapes that Helen had to deliver to 'Montelena,' because her husband Charles ran a full-time dental practice. Helen had given up her work as a pharmacist to manage the ranch. It took several trips over the mountains in her underpowered Volkswagen truck. To get up the steepest hills she would gun the engine on the flats and hope no one got in her way before she reached the top. The Bacigalupi family still grow grapes and starting with their third generation, they opened their own winery and tasting room, run by the twin granddaughters. The site of those original vines is on a low rise behind the tasting room. When I first visited years ago, they were still there and producing. But since then, the family replanted with new vines to support the next generation.

While that's a delightful story, the source of the rest of the grapes that went in those bottles is just as interesting. Most of the Chardonnay in Napa is grown in Los Carneros along the northern edge of the bay, with some good 'Chard' vineyards as far up as the Oak Knoll district, just south of Yountville. The upper valley is not only too hot, but it's so ideal for the expensive red Bordeaux grapes that Cabernet and Merlot take precedence.

The Napa vineyard where Mike Grgich found the rest of his Chard was at Muir Hanna, on the southwestern edge of Oak Knoll, at the foot of *basaltic* Mount Veeder. If the name Muir sounds familiar, then you may have visited Muir Woods, the famous redwood forest, a short ride up the coast from San Francisco.

John Muir was a naturalist and botanist whose research, lobbying efforts and friendship with President Theodore Roosevelt led to the establishment of the national parks system. We can thank him for Yosemite, which was the first National Park, and for founding the Sierra Club, a friend to tree lovers everywhere. His descendants farm a lovely vineyard in the southwest corner of Napa Valley just ten minutes from downtown.

I took clients there one day for a tasting having no idea of the family connection. But then I noticed two beautiful, period landscape paintings hanging on the wall in their living room. Being a lover of art, I asked them about the two scenes. That's when I found out who their great-grandfather was. Muir had mentored the painter, introducing him to Yosemite, and received the two paintings in thanks.

Was the 'Judgement' fair to the French, especially considering that a competition was not the original intention? It's true that Spurrier had included twice as many American wines as French, because he was anxious to show off what they had found on their trip to California. On the other hand, the tasting took place in Paris with all French judges, so the French wines enjoyed a home field advantage, or rather, a home palate advantage.

Based on their previous experiences, they could assume that the best wines were French. What they didn't figure on was the near ideal climatic and geologic conditions for growing wine grapes that the Americans enjoyed. The Californian's also had some very resolute and highly skilled people who believed in their vineyards' potential, and that was enough!

Did this 'Judgement' signal an immediate shift in the global wine world? *No!* The French, Italians and Germans were going to continue to buy the bottles that were filled down the lane from their homes, because that's what they had always done! But that article on the front page of the Times did tell the quickly growing number of American wine lovers, buyers and restaurants, that those guys and gals in California could make wines every bit as good as the French, at reasonable prices.

What they didn't foresee was that wine consumption the United States would almost *triple* since that time. They also didn't reckon on the effect that the American's dedication to research, technology and innovation would have on winemaking worldwide. The American's willingness to share that knowledge would gradually bend the standards that we use when we evaluate wine in their direction.

Above: Chateau Montelena
Opposite: A Crush Pad

Chapter Fourteen
How to Own a Winery *in 30 or So Steps*

Guests often ask us, "*Who owns the wineries?*"
Historically, the North Bay has mostly been home to small family vineyards and wineries. Mixed in with them are far fewer big production wineries, brands that you see on store shelves and restaurant wine lists.

The old farming families are the core of the region. The grandparents, or great grandparents paid a couple of hundred dollars an acre a hundred or more years ago and their families became tied to the land. They lived through the ups and downs of agriculture, planting grapes, plums, walnuts, olives and raising cattle and sheep, and always a kitchen garden. Now, after three or four generations their land is worth ten thousand times as much as their ancestors paid for it, and their grapes are in high demand. Someplace along the way they may have started making wine to sell. Depending on how early that decision was made, and how sensibly they carried it out, will tell you how wealthy they are now.

People often confuse the words vineyard and winery. The 'vine yard' is the land where the vines are planted and the grapes are harvested. It is a long-held belief that wines are made in the vineyard because the land's location and how it is managed determines the quality and nature of the wine.

The winery is where the harvested grapes are sent and put into tanks, where they ferment and become wine. From the time when it arrives at the crush pad, I've been told that there are thirty-two steps that a winemaker must perform to make the best possible wine from those grapes. So, we shouldn't underestimate the importance of the winery.

The big difference between the vineyard and the winery is this: Growing grapes is simple compared to operating a winery with its *expensive* technology, federal regulations and the need for highly trained, specialized staff. As a result, many more people own vineyards and sell their grapes, compared to those who operate wineries and sell the finished products. When you see the term Estate Winery on a label it means that they control the vineyards where the grapes are grown. In France the title *Vintner* covers both roles, but in California they are seen as quite different.

When it comes to winemakers, even though their name may be on a fancy wine bottle, if you scratch the surface, you often find a farmer underneath. Winemaking is a natural extension of farming, and both require long-term planning and patience. If they are lucky, a farm family will be large enough that the members with the aptitude for each role will rise to the challenge.

Many times, the first, and even second generation, are the ones out there on the tractor, but then someone in the next generation says, "Hey Mom and Dad, we should make some wine." To which their folks say, "UC Davis has a great winemaking program!" while thinking that a State School is a lot cheaper than the Ivy League. Also, if they go to school closer to home, there's a better chance they'll stay close to home when they finish.

Those smaller family wineries tend to be stable for a few reasons. First, and very importantly, the land has been paid off for years. Second, because generations grow up in the business, they know that it's *arduous* work requiring patience. The image of being a grape grower and vintner can seem idyllic, but it's *farming in the dirt*, subject to the weather, insects, changing market conditions and fires. It's not for the faint of heart. The third reason is that they are frugal, conservative in their thinking and suspicious of change.

For many of the old Italian American families the term 'testa dura,' for hardheaded, is an apt descriptor. Consider that it takes a year to prepare the land and plant the vineyard. Then you have to tend the vines for three years before you get the first harvest. But the premium growers won't use that young fruit, so they'll drop years number three and four on the ground. Finally in year five, six years after they started, they'll pick grapes that they can use or sell. It is a patient business!

Those qualities have served them well. A perfect example happened in the 1970's, a revolutionary time for the North Bay. A growing interest in wine fueled increased scientific focus on grape growing, and two approaches were introduced that affected the long-term economics. We need to first explain that many of the world's production grape vines are composed of two parts, merged with a graft. The upper *fruit stock* genetically comes from Europe. The *root stock* in the ground comes from the Americas. That's because there is a tiny American bug that lives in the soil, called phylloxera, which attacks the European vine's roots.

The popular Saint John's rootstock is native to the Americas and *resistant* to the bug. They started using it in the mid 1800's when the European vines were being widely planted in the Americas. Meanwhile, phylloxera spread to Europe and transformed the wine industry there, because they had to adopt the same grafting strategy to survive. In the process hundreds of traditional grape varieties were abandoned as growers with limited means prioritized grafting and replanting the most profitable varieties.

By the time the European vineyards were back on their feet, the overall acreage planted to wine grapes had *shrunk* dramatically. Saint John was a sturdy and dependable vine, but scientists felt they could do better.

In the 1970's they introduced the ARX root stock, reputed to deliver higher yields with good resistance. While many of the most modern, and successful wineries planted it, hoping to expand production, the hardheaded Italian families didn't. You can practically hear Papa saying to the kids who were urging him to spend the money for the new stock, *"My Nonno didn't use that, my Bisnonno didn't use that and we're not using that." That was the end of the discussion!*

About ten years after ARX was widely planted, phylloxera returned to those vineyards. The new root stock was not as resistant to the bug as advertised and the vines began to fail just when they should have been yielding a profit. This produced a string of wineries changing hands because they couldn't afford to replant. But the stubborn Italian family growers, as a local once told me, "...didn't lose a vine."

Another time where their hard heads kept them safe was when it came to *chemicals*. In the 1970's the thinking coming out of the Universities was that the growers should treat the soil like a growing medium. They could do everything with chemical fertilizers, insecticides, fungicides and whatever else the chemical companies had to sell. The biggest and most modern wineries jumped on board the chemical wagon while the old family wineries never left the sidewalk.

For them, tradition went hand in hand with convenience. Why? Because many of the family growers also raised cattle or had family members who did! They couldn't understand why they should pay for a chemical fertilizer when it fell out of the cows for free. As for gathering it up, *that's why they had kids.*

Today a problem that shows up in some of Napa's most valuable vineyards is called 'leaf curl,' where the vines lose photosynthesis because the leaves curl up. It shows up in the vineyards where they used those chemicals many years ago. Even when they've been converted to organic agriculture and replanted, the problem can persist for years. In Sonoma, an area dominated by Italian families, the problem is rare.

Since the time when Buena Vista started in the 1860's there has always been some large wineries in the North Bay. The Italian Swiss Colony Winery was a large operation. It was started in 1800's by a wealthy Italian banker who intended it to be a cooperative venture, where the workers would own a share. They eventually built a replica European tourist village in Northern Sonoma where families could spend the day, eating, drinking and playing. In the 1960's it was the *second biggest* tourist destination in California after Disneyland.

When Francis Ford Coppola, the famous movie director, opened his eponymous winery just minutes south of the former Italian Swiss Colony site, he followed the same model. The winery includes multiple restaurants, a film museum, a store, swimming pool with cabanas and bocce courts. Families can spend the day there, and there is something for all ages. Today most of the biggest wineries are in industrial looking buildings in the southern part of the counties. The wineries in the beautiful parts of the region have become valuable tourist destinations, although you can catch a glance of some of their large up-valley facilities if you know where to look. Driving north on Highway 29 in the Napa Valley, just past downtown Saint Helena, look for the historic Beringer Winery on your left.

Then immediately look to your right and you'll see, partially hidden behind trees and buildings, the lines of large stainless-steel tanks where their wines are made today. Over in Northern Sonoma, as you're driving north on Dry Creek Valley Road, approaching the old market at the intersection of Lambert Bridge Road, look to the right and you'll see the top of the tanks at Gallo's Northern Sonoma winemaking facility where they make a variety of labels.

The huge tanks form a double circle, around a central processing area. Both facilities take up plenty of acreage, but they are smaller than 'The Ranch,' an expansive facility on the south side of Zinfandel Lane in Rutherford between Highway 29 and the Silverado Trail. Take a peek at the site online with GPS maps, and you will get an idea of how big the wine business actually is! It's a thirsty world out there!

In the world of ultra-premium wines there are no 'large' wineries, which in the industry is defined as producing a million cases or more a year. Napa's Robert Mondavi Winery, the *incredibly* popular V. Sattui, the historic Beaulieu Vineyards and the revered Joseph Phelps in Napa, as well as Sonoma's venerable Kunde Family, biodynamic Benziger, and the widely distributed Saint Francis and Chateau Saint Jean don't come close.

The limiting factor for premium wineries is being able to find enough grapes of the required quality. While California produces loads of machine farmed and harvested wine grapes, the amount of hand pruned, picked and sorted fruit, from ideal locations, is small in comparison. It's also challenging to find enough skilled labor to do that work. Finally, you need people willing to take the financial risk of investing in a project with a limited market.

Grape growing families like Beringer, Martini, Sebastiani, La Tour, Mondavi, Benziger, Duncan, Gallo and Boisset, came here to make wine. Almost half of those came here from another country and stayed because they recognized the specialness of the place, not only its agricultural potential, but its proximity to markets.

After the old farming families and the grape growers, the next group of wineries were started by the ship captains who came here to transport those farm products. They primarily founded wineries in the Napa Valley, because unlike the Sonoma Valley, Napa has a navigable river. They saw it as the perfect place to build the kind of palatial wineries that they had seen in Europe.

These were worldly men, entrepreneurial to the core and accustomed to navigating risks successfully. This kind of daring and determined personality has always gravitated to Napa, all the way back to mountain men like George Yount, who planted the first Napa grapes. Why did the valley appeal to these sea going men more than Sonoma? Probably because Napa Valley is expansive, with a wide, level floor, where you can see for miles! That would please men who had spent years on the ocean, where they only felt truly safe when the wind was following, the sea was friendly, and the horizons were free of threats.

In a fascinating repetition of a community of wealthy entrepreneurs from a specific industry arriving in the North Bay, a hundred years later the Silicon Valley engineers arrived, looking for a place to invest. The computer manufacturing center is just a couple of hours south of Napa and Sonoma, and for many years the North Bay has been a favorite spot for them to relax and play.

They called it *'Silicon Valley's Back Yard.'* The beauty of the place appealed to them, as did the wine-making technology. While historically European wine-making was the province of the Church and landed aristocracy, several events in the 1970's and 1980's made wineries an attractive place for entrepreneurs to invest.

In the premium wine world, the safest place to put money is in the red Bordeaux grapes, Cabernet Sauvignon, Cabernet Franc, Merlot, Malbec and Petite Verdot. This is because they age so well that their value increases over time. We call them the *'banker's wines'* and they tend to be a favorite of people in the finance world, and not just because they are expensive.

Compared to California, France has a short growing season. When they harvest these grapes, the tannins are quite high, so they are aged for four or five years to allow the tannins to soften and make the wine palatable and ready to sell. For an engineer that's a long time. It's common for their projects to take two years from start to market, so five years was a not an attractive timeline. But, in the North Bay, the bright sunshine and long growing season allows the tannins to break down on the vine before they are harvested, shortening the amount of aging time required. That by itself could make all the difference but then, the wine world rediscovered the importance of barrels. For centuries European wines were made and stored in wooden barrels.

But, there was not much attention paid to the influence of the wood on the wine. It was simply the easiest material to work with, and transport, and the oak and chestnut barrels were used until they wore out. It got worse after WWII, when the war disrupted both the wineries and the coopers who made the barrels. Thanks to the American Marshall Plan for rebuilding Europe, many wineries abandoned barrels in favor of *concrete* tanks. I've often described the Marshall Plan as a system by which the USA loaned Europe money to pay American companies to pour concrete for them, including the construction of lots of winemaking tanks.

The pivotal event was when the new head of Chateau Margaux, who had done his university dissertation about how oak barrels affect wine, installed a new barrel program at the winery. They found that the barrels softened the wine, in part by converting the malic acid to lactic acid, and it accelerated the process of making the wine palatable.

In the United States Jess Jackson of Kendall Jackson, a self-made San Francisco native, was one of the early American advocates for oak barrels. He created a unique style of wine that has proven exceedingly popular when he put his chardonnay into new oak barrels. It produced a buttery, oaky wine, with vanilla, caramel and chocolate flavors and it is still a big seller.

I've never heard anyone else discuss this, but I have a background as a professional herbalist and perfumer, and there is something I've noticed that explains this style of wine's success. It has to do with that unique combination of flavors and mouth feel. It is similar to one of America's favorite beverages, something that teenagers of a certain generation lived on, Coca Cola.

The thing about flavors and scents is that the body never forgets them. They are stored in the part of the brain where emotions live, and when we recognize the flavors, we recall the emotions. When new wine drinkers tasted Kendall Jackson's signature chardonnay, their palates recognized that 'recipe' and it brought up familiar emotions of carefree times with their young friends. *Suddenly they were surprised that they liked wine so much!*

How successful was Jess's strategy? By the time he passed away in his eighties, his family owned over forty premium and ultra-premium wineries, and they were one of the two largest buyers of wine grapes in Sonoma! Today's oak barrel industry, which was almost moribund at the end of World War Two, is a raging, international success!

Let's look at an example from Napa. The Silver Oak Winery has four locations. In Napa, the Oakville winery specializes in Cabernet blends while the Calistoga winery, called Twomey, makes Merlot. In Sonoma, the state of the art Silver Oak Winery in the broad Alexander Valley makes the Cabernet Blend, while the Russian River Twomey, in another remarkable building, makes Pinot Noir and Chardonnay. The Silver Oak Cabernets are tremendously popular, especially with a younger palate.

What's their secret? *There are two!* First, rather than getting their grapes from the hillside vineyards that produce more complex flavors, the Silver Oak Winery favors valley floor fruit, with its more fulsome profile. Second, while most of their neighbors favor the more expensive French oak barrels with their tight grain, Silver Oak is so dedicated to the American barrels, with their rounder vanilla and nutty flavors, that they have their own forest and barrel facility.

Now, the Silicon Valley engineers realized that North Bay Cabernet, if given enough time on the vine to soften its tannins and enrich its flavors, was then put in new oak barrels, *they could sell the bottles in two years.* If they held onto the bottles for a while, they would keep getting better and more valuable.

For those engineers, a two-year timeline from harvest to market was something with which they were comfortable. Also, they normally manufactured products that suffered from quick obsolescence. The fact that the cellared wine would grow in value was a positive change. Finally, those bottles would have their names on them. No one ever got to put their name on a computer chip!

In the early 1970's, when there were about twenty old-time wineries in Napa, and thirty in Sonoma, there was a burst of new wineries that came on the scene that today are among the most renowned. That was surprising considering that the technology was far from state-of-the-art. The roads were narrow, with gravel shoulders, if they had shoulders at all. There were no great restaurants or fancy hotels. Everyone drove pickup trucks and there were more cowboy hats than business suits. The area produced apples, plums, walnuts and wine grapes. While those grapes were grown in Napa and Sonoma, they were shipped to big wineries outside the counties and put into reasonably priced bottles with an array of popular names.

Ever since Prohibition, California had focused on quantity, not quality. Then three things happened concurrently. First, the California Agriculture Bureau told anyone who would listen that they could grow world-class grapes in California, especially in Napa and Sonoma. Second, a generation of college students traveled in Europe and enjoyed the wonderful wine culture there.

While their parents enjoyed cocktails and beer, they wanted something different. *San Francisco had plenty of folks of that new generation,* who were, coincidentally enjoying a great deal of prosperity from the expansion of the Pacific Rim markets.

People from the city began investing in the North Bay vineyards. This way, when they went to parties in the city, they could tell people that, "yes, I am an attorney, but my real passion is growing grapes." If you added a slightly rugged dress jacket to your wardrobe, so much the better. Now that would be enough to inspire growth but fortunately, the state legislators were listening to the agricultural agencies, so they decided to do something about this opportunity. *Guess what? They liked drinking wine too!*

They created a financial incentive for farmers who planted wine grapes. That helped the growers and vintners buy the equipment they needed. But it gets better! Napa County had recently voted to create America's first Agricultural Preserve. This protected the valley from the proposed construction of a multilane highway, and hillsides filled with housing developments. It was a hotly contested initiative, but the benefit was considerable. True, it restricted the way that owners could use their land, but if they used it for farming or ranching, their taxes would be kept low.

The combination of these three factors led to the founding of some of the North Bay's favorite wineries: Stag's Leap Cellars, Clos Du Bois, Chateau Montelena, Far Niente, Caymus and Darioush. In Sonoma, even without becoming a preserve, wineries like Chateau Saint Jean, Benziger, Ferrari Carano and Jordan appeared on the scene. They collectively got a tremendous boost when two of these wineries, Stag's Leap Wine Cellars and Chateau Montelena, triumphed in the Judgment of Paris blind tasting in 1976.

Throughout the history of this region, it has benefited from infusions of cheap labor. Starting in the 1850's Chinese workers arrived and found work clearing vineyards, building walled enclosures from the native stone, and digging wine caves. The region's many Italian families got their foot in the door when thousands of their young men arrived in the late 1800's, ready to work. They left Italy when their own wine industry collapsed due to the arrival of phylloxera and years of drought.

Starting in the 1970's, when the shift to premium wines began, the annual arrival of Mexican fruit pickers, resulted in the local wineries holding onto some of them as full-time workers. Today, in the North Bay vineyards, Spanish is spoken more often than English, and the premium winery industry would be *impossible* without the Mexican workers and their families.

Just like the Italians before them, the children of those original Mexican farm workers have become managers, winemakers and vineyard owners. When your family started here by working in the fields, the next generation was taught to appreciate the opportunities so much more.

Finally, there are wealthy people who want a home in the vineyard as part of their *bucket list*. They purchase vineyards as investments, which double as vacation homes. Putting it together from scratch requires deep pockets and the willingness to hire the correct experts. You start with a real estate agent who specializes in vineyards and wineries. They in turn help you find a vineyard consultant to plan the vineyard, who will help you find a vineyard management company to plant and farm the vines. Then you need an architect and construction company to build your home and winery. They recommend an attorney to handle the winery permits, and once you make wine, the compliance documents.

Hopefully, your vineyard consultant will recommend a consulting winemaker. If they don't your neighbors will. They will work with your architect to select your winemaking equipment and find an assistant winemaker/cellarmaster, who will do the daily work under the consultant's direction. Of course, until your own winery is constructed, your consulting winemaker will find you a custom crush facility to process the grapes you're going to buy while you wait for your own grapes to be ready in five years. If you are going to do all that, then why not dig a cave? It will save you money in the long term, and this is about saving money, isn't it?

The architect will design the cave and find you an excavation company that will manage the incredibly complex dance of timing that process. You will need a designer and printer for your labels. Your winemaker will purchase the bottles and eventually, you will need an estate manager to host guests, sell your wine and manage the wine club.

If you really want to get your winery's name out there, you'll pay the estate manager to travel around the country doing tastings for wealthy customers. There are plenty of properties like this in the North Bay where the home is only used a few weeks each year. But there is a benefit. During holidays, the wine on your family's table has your name on the label.

If you want your own winery, you don't have to work your way through this considerable list of professionals and businesses. *You can simply buy an operating winery estate.* There are plenty of those for sale,

where the original person who went through that complete process was three or four owners back. I've seen
numerous people build wineries, intending them as a
legacy for their family, but then, when their kids inher-
ited the property, they didn't want the work or responsi-
bility. *Wineries look glamourous, especially when you
are sitting on a high patio with a glass in your hand,* but
vines grow in the dirt and, at their heart, this is farming
and food production. Although, I admit, wineries can be
an especially elegant expression of those arts.

Northern Napa Wineries in the 1800's

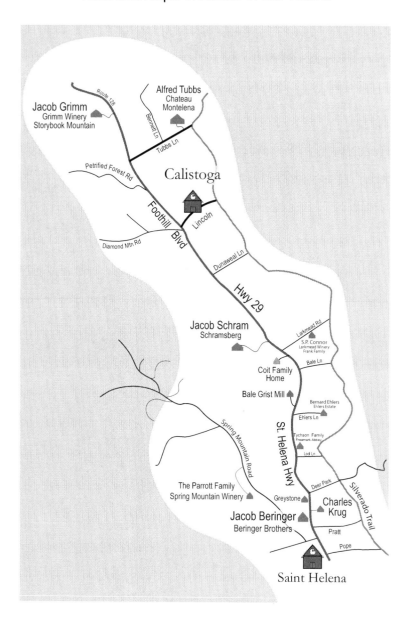

Opposite: Charles Krug Winery

Chapter Fifteen
The Story of the Three Jakes

They say that the story of Northern Napa starts with the story of the three Jakes, Prussian winemakers who arrived in Napa in the 1870's. To best tell their story we need to provide some context. When the first settlers arrived in any new land, they always claimed the properties near the waterways. That location came with advantages; first was water for irrigation, but equally important for the budding entrepreneurs, was easy access to the docks where ships brought needed supplies. That was also where farmers and craftsmen might find ship captains looking for goods they could ship. Those dockside areas eventually became places of commerce and fortunes were made by the owners of warehouses where the deals were struck between the farmers and the shippers.

The farther that each group settled from the docks, the longer and more expensive their route to the market. The Napa River runs the length of the county, but the location of the city, which was the northernmost place that a ship could reach, is at the bottom of the valley. Above that, an oxbow-shaped bend, with its undulating banks and shallows, makes passage impossible.

The oldest building in the valley, a beautifully restored adobe, belonged to a Sergeant in the Mexican army. It sits at the junction of the Silverado Trail and Soscol Avenue, once known as the 'Old Soscol Ferry Road.' All the land that the Sergeant could see was his, thanks to a land grant in gratitude for his service. He sold a *patch* of land to an American also named Jacob.

Jacob Coombs established downtown Napa, one of the first 'American' cities in California. He in turn sold land to other Americans and they wasted no time establishing the docks. Some of the oldest houses in that part of town were built by ship captains who transported produce from the valley to San Francisco and beyond. Once the docks opened optimistic settlers came from around the world, especially the French, Prussian and Italian winemakers. One of the most revered was the first of the winemaking Jakes, Jacob Beringer.

He and his brother Frederick had arrived in New York City to make beer for America's growing population. But Jacob, the younger brother and winemaker, heard about the wonderful wine grapes being grown in the North Bay region, so the brothers decided he should check the place out. If it looked like a sound investment,

Frederick, the money guy, would find investors in New York City.

Mark Twain has a wonderful commentary about who comes to California, *"America is built on a tilt, and everything loose eventually rolls to the Pacific."* The North Bay, more than most places, has benefitted from the efforts of big personalities, who coincidentally were often the youngest boys in the family. Why are the youngest children so often adventurers? Because traditionally, in European cultures, inheritance passed to the oldest son, so the younger siblings could either work for their elder brother or make their own way. Since the youngest son had the least to lose and were often accustomed to making their own way, that was who you often found on the frontiers where opportunity and risk co-existed.

So, Jake Beringer, the younger brother, headed to the frontier. When he arrived in Napa, he got a job working at the Charles Krug Winery. Krug was a Prussian socialist writer and philosopher, who had established his winery far from the river docks for a couple of reasons.

First, much of the best growing land to the south had already been grabbed by the Americans. Second, and more importantly, Krug had married the daughter of the notorious, quarrelsome and quite colorful Dr. Edward Bale. The young Miss Bale's dowry included several hundred acres of potentially prime farmland just north of downtown Saint Helena, which today is the site of Napa's oldest existing winery, Charles Krug, owned by the Mondavi family.

Bale was an English ship's physician who had been shipwrecked off the coast of Monterey at the sudden conclusion of his first voyage. He had fallen into a fortuitous position as the doctor to the Spanish Governor, because the previous physician had recently led a *revolt* against the Governor and now was persona non grata. As part of his duties, he served as the physician for the Presidio in San Francisco where he was known for producing remedies with a *remarkably* high amount of alcohol. This did not endear him to some of the local women, who were having a hard enough time managing the wild men who were drawn to this remote outpost, without the Doctor's nefarious potions.

However, that position led to him marrying General Vallejo's niece and being given a sizable land grant in Northern Napa, where he is known locally for funding the building of the *Bale Grist Mill*, outside Saint Helena. Bale also, for some weird reason, named his land grant 'Carne Humana,' or human flesh. He didn't stick around to explain, because when gold was discovered in the Sierra Madre Mountains, he *headed for the hills* and met his demise there.

Before starting his winery, Charles Krug worked for Count Haraszthy at Buena Vista in Sonoma, where he learned winemaking. The Count loaned Krug a small apple press to get him started. Krug neglected to return it and you can see it at Krug's Winery, built in the late 1800's. On the very entertaining historic tour at Buena Vista, the Count, recently portrayed by an actor in an ambassadorial role, seems to be especially pained by

Krug's oversight and the loss of his prodigal press. While Krug was the owner for only a brief time, his name is enshrined on Napa's oldest winery still in existence.

So, while Jacob Beringer worked for Krug, his brother Fredrick was making beer in New York City and pursuing that most 'New York-esque' of goals; raising money for the California winery his brother was envisioning. Eventually the brothers purchased land across the road from Krug and in 1876 built their winery on a slope above the road at the northern edge of downtown Saint Helena. They could reach the Napa River docks via the railroad tracks that ran the length of the valley. This made shipping their wine easy.

The Beringer Winery has the distinction of having *never missed a harvest*, even during Prohibition when they made wine for the churches, although they did hide bottles to avoid the 'unreasonable' taxes. They promptly forgot about that, because many years later, while doing repairs in the cave, they found caches of wine bottles hidden in walled up niches.

While Jacob Beringer was making a success within walking distance from the pretty town of Saint Helena, farther north outside Calistoga, the second Jake, Jacob Schram, was *'hoeing a harder row.'* Schram was a Prussian barber and winemaker who married a good German American girl, Annie Weaver. They were building the Schramsberg Winery, high on the slopes of the Mayacamas Mountain range, in an area known as Diamond Mountain. Even today, driving up the hill in a car, it's a steep climb from the valley floor. I can only imagine the number of curses that the trees along that drive heard, as wagons hauled loads of supplies up the mountain behind their straining teams of oxen and horses.

Being on the hills so far north brought an advantage. Hillsides made of volcanic ash are perfect for digging extensive caves for aging the wine. That backbreaking and dangerous kind of work was done by the Chinese miners who had been digging silver and mercury on the slopes of Mount Saint Helena and in the hills of Sonoma's Alexander Valley.

The Beringer wineries were built against the hillsides to accommodate a cave as well, but they don't compare to the deep caverns that have been bored into the hills behind the Schramsberg Winery. Clearly Jacob and Annie were bold thinkers, willing to take a risk and industrious enough to make it work.

In Northern Napa there was a wealthy San Francisco family called Coit. They owned a beautiful ranch that spanned from the Mayacamas to the west, across the valley floor and up into the Vaca hillsides to the east. This was just a short distance from the Schram winery. Their daughter, Lillie Coit, was a *San Fransico icon*. She was known as 'Fire Bell Lil,' because she was both the darling and the patroness of the San Francisco fire companies, who had saved her life several times. She was one of early San Francisco's great personalities.

Like many well-to-do city families, they had a home outside the foggy city to get away from the cold and damp and enjoy the warm summer sun in Napa. The Coit Ranch was quite the gathering place where renowned authors and prominent locals were often invited to socialize. In the days before television and the internet, if you can imagine such a time, card games were often featured in these gatherings.

Not surprisingly, their guests often included the local winemakers, who would always arrive with a bottle or two of their best wines. One night Jacob Schram and Jacob Beringer were engaged in a friendly game of poker in the Coit parlor. They were both holding good hands, and Jacob Schram bet two large, ornately carved winemaking tanks. But Lady Luck was smiling on Jacob Beringer that evening, and a couple of days later the two tanks, with the name Schramsberg, meaning Schram's Mountain, carved on the front, arrived on a wagon at the Beringer winery. They stayed there in the winery for almost *one hundred years.*

Now while the Beringer family managed to keep their very conveniently situated winery until the 1970's, the Schrams didn't endure the scourge of phylloxera as well, and the winery sat closed for many years. Finally, in 1965, the Davies family bought the property and began the slow process of bringing it back to life. In a surprise decision for the time, they decided to focus on producing sparkling wines by the traditional Méthode Champenoise under the name Schramsberg. About the same time, the Beringer family was in discussions to sell the winery to the Swiss food giant, Nestle.

As Chapter two of Jacob and Annie Schram's winery began with the new owners, there were only about twenty wineries in the valley. This was dramatically different from Jacob's time when there were over a hundred. In the 1960's, with so few wineries, if you were so inclined you could visit each one and expect a nice reception. Jaime Davies did just that, visiting her neighbors to learn what she could about the local wine business. Of course, she had to visit Jacob Beringer's Winery, where she was shown around by the head winemaker, Ed Sbragia, a big, friendly guy who grew up in Geyserville in Northern Sonoma.

They were walking through the caves and came upon these two, tall wooden tanks with the name Schramsberg carved on their faces. Jaime must have been a little shocked to see those two tanks, which were so obviously from 'her' winery, there in the Beringer cellar. She asked Ed about the tanks, and he told her about the card game between the two Jakes at Lillie Coit's house, and about who had the better hand.

By this time, almost a hundred years later the tanks were veritable antiques, and no longer usable for winemaking, but they were part of her winery's history. So, she asked Ed if she could buy them, but Ed said sorry, no! Jaime thought, 'That was that!' What she didn't know was that Beringer was about to close the deal with Nestle. Ed didn't want to have to say to the new owners, "Oh, those tanks weren't included in the price." More importantly, one of the qualities that made it an attractive deal for the Swiss was the Beringer history. When they took over, they worked hard to turn it into a major tourist destination with an extensive menu of historical tours.

Once the deal was completed, and Jacob Beringer's winery started its second chapter with the new owners, Jaime got a phone call from Ed Sbragia's secretary, who said, "Ed would like to invite you to a card game at the winery. You'll be *playing for those tanks* with the Schramsberg name on the front. Jaime's initial reaction was something like 'What on earth is this about?' But Jaime said she would be happy to come, and the secretary gave her a date and time, and suggested that she wear something nice.

A few weeks later Jaime showed up at the appointed time and place and there, on the broad walkway, in front of the winery was a card table, with all the accoutrements. Next to it, lit up like a stage set, were the two tanks, freshly cleaned and polished. Ed Sbragia and his assistant winemakers were here and there chatting with some photographers and Nestle executives.

Jaime had just *walked into a publicity event* designed to celebrate the colorful history of the winery. It seemed great to Jaime since she would get the tanks for free, but there was one hitch. She confided in Ed that she had never played poker in her life, so she was a little unsure about how she was going the win the jackpot. Ed reassured her saying, "Don't worry about it, you just *play the cards that we deal you.*" He had stacked the deck for her, so the tanks, after so many years away, would be going home.

The tour at Schramsberg has become one of our favorites because of its history, its unique aging caves with their stacked bottles stretching into the mountainside, and the natural beauty of the place. Today, when you take the tour of their caves the oversized pair of tanks sit side by side in a place of honor, looking quite happy to be back where they belong.

This was not the only time that luck figured into the wineries fate. Two events dramatically helped the winery cement its fortunes. In the late 1800's when Robert Louis Stevenson and his American bride Fanny honeymooned in Calistoga, the local stagecoach driver, Long John Silverado, brought them there for a visit. The young couple were thoroughly impressed by what the Schram's had accomplished, especially considering that Jacob, a Prussian immigrant, had been a barber with a shop in downtown Saint Helena.

He and Annie chose this hillside land because it was cheap enough that they could afford it. This was a different situation from Jacob Beringer with his financier brother. Schram's rag to riches story on the far frontier so appealed to Stevenson that their winery was memorialized in his book, 'The Silverado Squatters,' which gained them some much appreciated attention.

Another stroke of luck happened a hundred years later, and it made a dramatic difference to the reborn winery's eventual success. In 1972, President Nixon and his Secretary of State, Henry Kissinger, organized an unannounced trip to open a diplomatic relationship with China. Nixon wanted to bring an American sparkling wine for the banquet. He was from California and wanted an American owned, California wine, of which there were very few, but luckily Nixon was familiar with

Schramsberg. So, Jaime gets a phone call from some guy at the State Department, explaining that they would like to buy twenty cases of their best 'Champagne.' What Jaime didn't tell him was that twenty cases would be *one fifth of the winery's production* that year. But happy for the sale, the winery folks loaded up a truck and drove over the eastern hills to Travis Airforce Base, where a crew put the wine on a plane and flew it to Washington DC. They eventually received the payment from the State Department, thank you very much!

But then, a few weeks later, the fireworks went off when Nixon and Kissinger landed in China! One of Jaime's friends called her on the phone and said, "Turn on the TV, Barbara Walters is in Tiananmen Square in Peking (as Beijing was known in the west at the time) holding up a bottle of your wine." Schramsberg gained instant fame in the wine world, for being part of this historic event, with the greatest endorsement possible. Not surprisingly, they sold out that entire year's production, and the next and the next, and their name became synonymous with great California sparkling wines.

While Jacob Beringer built his winery just outside the town of Saint Helena, and Jacob and Annie Schram built their estate just south of downtown Calistoga, the third Jake, named Jacob Grimm, yes, like the fairy tale author, built his winery north of Calistoga. He bought hillside land in a remote location, on the road to Sonoma's Knight's Valley. It had to be dirt cheap, but it was well chosen, because like the other two Jakes, he chose western hillsides for his winery, so the vines could take advantage of the morning sunshine. While Jacob Grimm had the longest ride the docks, *he also had the most beautiful views of Mount Saint Helena.* From the property today you can still see the old mine tailings on the slopes of that graceful mountain.

The winery is on a part of the road that has more winding sections than straight, and the entrance to Grimm's property is on rise. From there the land rises again on a gentle slope leading to a small hollow, where Jacob and his brother built the Grimm winery. From there the hillside rises steeply, so they cut trellises to plant the vines.

Unlike the vintners of Oakville, Rutherford and Saint Helena, with their nice level vineyards, the process of cutting trellises into hillsides, and farming those inclines can be back breaking work. This was in the days before ATV's, rototillers, tractors, backhoes and bulldozers. But the work paid off and the vineyards thrived, producing wonderful grapes for *almost a hundred years.*

Like the other two Prussian Jakes, Grimm brought in the Chinese hard rock miners to cut caves into the volcanic hills behind the crush pad, which are still used today. When you go inside it feels a little eerie because the walls are coated with a non-toxic mold that lines many of the ancient French caves. Even though they tell you it's not dangerous, there is something in human psychology that is cautious about mold and fungus.

Grimm farmed these beautiful, terraced hillsides for many years. While the winery eventually closed, the vineyards kept producing until the early 1960's, when a fire raging across the northern part of the county raced through the vineyards, reducing the vines and buildings to ash.

It was after that when a college history professor visited the denuded, terraced hill and decided that this would be a good place to raise his family and make wine. Realizing that he didn't know enough about the land, he hired the most prominent consultant in the area, the diminutive Russian André Tchelistcheff. André was the winemaker at both Beaulieu Vineyards and Buena Vista, and he laid out many of the region's most interesting vineyards.

André walked the hills and told the new owner that this land was *perfect for Zinfandel.* Now today, if any Napa consultant told a new vineyard owner that they should plant Zin they'd be fired. Half of the grapes in Napa today are of the 'big bucks' Cabernet Sauvignon variety, but it wasn't always like that. At one time Zinfandel and Petite Sirah were the dominant red grapes and the northern part of the valley especially enjoyed the steady heat that Zin adores. For growers, Zinfandel has the advantage of ripening early and producing a good red, medium bodied wine. In a competitive market, an early ripening grape can help a grower get to the market when there are more buyers who are looking to buy fruit and have pockets full of money.

All during the thirteen years of Prohibition, Italian immigrants on the East Coast and along the Great Lakes bought grapes for their homemade wines, and Zin was one of the four best shipping grapes. That's why north of the narrow neck of the Napa Valley, where the town of Saint Helena is located, there are still plenty of Zinfandel vines, distinctive due to their lack of trellises. But to get back to the Grimm Vineyards, based on what André recommended, the Professor and his family planted Zinfandel and five other varieties that would grow well there.

Besides marketability, there was a practical benefit that the selection produced. Because each variety ripened at a different time, and their location on the hillside further extended that timeline, they could harvest the entire sixty acres of vineyards over three months, with just four men. On that steep hillside they depend on small ATV's and twenty-five-pound picking bins. They cart the grapes down the hill to where the Professor, now the winemaker, personally *tips the bins* into the tanks, making sure that every grape is as perfect as possible.

In an interesting confirmation of André's assessment, in recent years the scientists from the University of California at Davis, one of the world's most esteemed winemaking colleges, came by with an offer. They had solved a long-time problem that Zinfandel suffers from, uneven ripening in the bunches, using a new clone they developed. In viticulture a clone is a natural mutation that develops from an existing vine. The leaves, fruit or root will exhibit different qualities from the mother plant. The growers will propagate it, to see if it has desirable properties. If it does, it may eventually replace the other vines in the field. All the vines you see in the vineyards today are clones, of clones, of clones, as growers sought better and better vines.

For generations Zinfandel growers had sought solutions to the problem of unripe, bitter grapes in bunches that were otherwise ready to be made into wine. When they threw in the entire bunches, those tart berries would affect the flavor. If they kept the grapes on the vine until the bunches were entirely ripe, the higher sugar levels produced *ballistic* alcohol that would dry out your palate with each sip. The third solution is a method used by high-end wineries, where the bunches are de-stemmed and the grapes are sorted individually, an expensive and labor-intensive way to eliminate those unripe berries.

The scientists at UC Davis had produced a Zinfandel clone where the bunches ripened evenly, and they wanted to plant a test vineyard, which would later belong to the winery. Why did they come to the Professor? Because they had determined that this was the best location in California for growing Zinfandel! Andre was right!

Jacob Grimm would have been pleased to see the dedication that his vineyards inspired, and the owner wanted to name it for him, calling it *the Grimm Winery*. That's not a surprising thought from a former history professor. But his children *overruled* him and after some discussion they chose something that connected the place to the third Prussian Jake, Storybook Mountain.

A Still in Wine Country

Chapter Sixteen
Prohibition Stories

When you live in an area where the industry revolves around wine, anything that affects the legality, acceptance, or even opinion about alcohol sends ripples through the community. Even today, when a state changes their shipping requirements to make it easier for wineries to ship their products, it's immediately in the industry news. How much then did prohibition affect Wine Country? That's when the United States of America decided that after thousands of years of wine serving humanity so faithfully, alcohol consumption should be *illegal!* That affected the North Bay dramatically, on multiple levels and it left behind some interesting stories!

One of my *favorites* is about the Nichelini family, who have owned their winery in the far part of Napa's Chiles Valley for five generations. I've often thought of how poor, but determined those folks must have been to homestead in such a difficult place. The Chiles is a narrow valley surrounded by steep hillsides, and the old winery is perched on a ridge by the side of a narrow road. From the Silverado Trail, it's a 20-minute ride in a modern car up winding Sage Canyon Road just to reach them. How hard was it to establish a winery there when they depended on oxen and mule carts?

But even though it's a difficult location, it did have one big advantage. It is on the road that connects the heart of the Napa Valley, east through the hills to the Central Valley and the State Capitol of Sacramento. The other route from the upper valley takes you south through the city of Napa and around the mountains, which lengthens the trip considerably.

Back in the day, for people traveling through those narrow passes, the *only place to stop for lunch* was at Mrs. Nichelini's. She didn't cook anything custom, just served whatever she was making that day. But since this is Napa and everything grows well here, you could count on it being a satisfying meal. In the early years of prohibition, the local police occasionally ignored minor infractions, but the federal revenue agents were another matter. One day, two revenue agents were traveling from Sacramento to Napa, and they stopped in at Mrs. Nichelini's for lunch. The Missus put out a wonderful meal for them and being a good Italian-Swiss wife, Caterina put out two glasses of wine for the gentlemen. The two Revenue Agents enjoyed their meal, paid her, said thank you very much, and then *arrested* her for bootlegging.

Now this is farm country, where everybody knows everybody and people were incensed that they would arrest her, a friend and a mother. Of course, there was also the practical consideration of lunch. If she was in jail, there wasn't going to be any place to stop for food on the road back-and-forth to Sacramento. It caused such an uproar that the local Justice had to find a better solution.

So instead, they arrested her husband, Anton Nichelini, who was a bit of a hard case. That was seen as a better, although not ideal solution. The locals had suffered economic devastation due to this crazy law, so people felt that sending him to prison was completely unfair. So, the judge decided that he should serve his six-month term in the local jail, a short distance from his home.

The local sheriff wasn't happy about this either, so Anton wasn't *locked* in a cell. Instead, he helped around the place during the day. The fact that he shared the care packages from his wife's kitchen didn't hurt. There was one logistical problem, the sheriff didn't work weekends, so Anton would go home to his wife and a pile of chores. For an industrious farmer and miner like him, his six-month term was the closest thing he ever got to a vacation. Hopefully, they timed it for the winter when the vines were asleep, because his neighbors depended on him for grapes and bottles of good wine.

My *second favorite* story from prohibition is about how Samuele Sebastiani, whose winery was a short walk from the Sonoma Plaza, ingeniously dealt with this potential disaster. Sam had built his winery in 1906, so by the time prohibition happened in late 1919 he was well-established. The first thing he did in reaction to this horrible news was to fill out the application to make wine for the Catholic churches and the Jewish Temples. Like most Italian immigrants, he was a devoted Catholic and those services include wine, in memory of Jesus's first miracle, turning water into wine.

Yes, according to the Bible, *Jesus was a wine-maker!* There are also numerous parables about tending vineyards including the story of Adam and Eve. When their sons, Cain and Abel went looking for work, one became a shepherd while the other tended vines. What kind of vines do you think those were? If the government attempted to restrict the use of wine by the churches and temples, they would have been interfering with their freedom of religion, the bedrock upon which America was founded. So that's not happening!

Over in Napa, George LaTour, the owner of Beaulieu Vineyards, also got the permit to make wine for the churches. But *he had a special connection!* Just up the road was a large estate owned by the arch diocese of San Francisco, and George was friends with the archbishop. The church would send troubled kids from the city to work on the farm. Today that property is owned by the Round Pond Winery, and as you travel across Rutherford Road you can see the old chapel left behind from those days. George asked the archbishop for a letter of introduction to parishes in need of sacramental wine throughout the country.

While all of La Tour's neighbor wineries closed, except for Beringer and Christian Brothers, a religious brotherhood, Beaulieu Vineyards expanded. While Prohibition was hard on Wine Country, it was *fantastic* financially for the churches and temples, where membership boomed. There were reports of Jewish temples in New York City that grew five times over, and they suddenly included many new families named O'Donnell, O'Leary and Murphy.

But to get back to Sam Sebastiani, at a time when many people were ripping out vines and planting the Italian plum trees used for prunes, Sam and his friends were buying up vineyards. That's because Prohibition happened during the second great wave of Italian migration to the United States. The first wave started in the late 1800's, the second started after the First World War and the third took place in the 1960's.

Most people don't realize that the Italians were one of the *single largest migrations* ever to come to the United States. Sixty million Italians came in three great waves and pizza has been one of America's favorite foods ever since. Amazingly, more Italians left their country for the Americas than live in Italy today. Many of them settled along the East Coast and the shores of the Great Lakes and while some of them were winemakers, all were wine drinkers. When I was growing up in New Jersey, where forty percent of the population was descended from Italy, I used to hear, *"All those old Italians make wine"!* It turns out they were right. That's because, starting in the 1800s, phylloxera attacked the Italian vines and the wine industry, which employed 80% of working people, mostly collapsed. Anyone who could leave the country did, looking for work!

When Congress passed the law banning alcohol, they made a cut out for the home winemaker, I think in part because of the large numbers of Italians, who were a pretty tough lot and many of them carried knives! At first the wine could only have about 1% alcohol, but that lasted about five minutes, and they quickly raised it to a more reasonable 8% to 9%, but with the home winemakers, who was checking? Every neighborhood had their local winemaker. *I know this because* my grandfather was his community's winemaker and he made wine for them for over 40 years. During prohibition, a local winemaker would gather the names of the families they were making wine for, and each could get up to *two hundred* gallons per year, which is a lot of wine. My father, who was my grandfather's youngest child, told me about going down to the rail lines in the Iron Bound section of Newark with his father, to buy boxes upon boxes of grapes.

Before going to school in the morning, he and his brothers did the punch downs where they would push the floating grapes down into the juice, to infuse it with flavor and color. In the off season, they would take the barrels apart, clean and reassemble them. Even back then, good winemaking was mostly about cleanliness, and having five sons was a big advantage.

Meanwhile, back in California, Samuele Sebastiani, along with the Mondavis and the Gallos, recognized that these winemakers, their fellow Italians, would need grapes. So, while the Americans were tearing out vines, the Italian Americans were planting more, and during prohibition, wine grape production in Sonoma tripled.

So now, besides making church wine, Sam was shipping grapes to the East Coast. You would think that this just allowed them to survive, but in fact Prohibition was a boon to the Italian American growers, because the home winemakers at the other end of that rail line, would pay more for grapes than their local wineries had ever paid. By the time Prohibition ended the Italian American growers owned extensive vineyards in prime locations throughout the state and those Italian American families have *dominated* the California wine industry since then.

But making wine for the churches and shipping grapes wasn't the only part of Sam's Prohibition strategy. When he made wine for the churches, the alcohol was taxed immediately. On the day when the grapes were put in the tank, the taxman would come by. They would calculate the volume of juice, and the amount of sugar, and from those amounts they would determine how much alcohol was going to be made. They would calculate the tax and Sam would write the check and the taxman would leave. What the tax man didn't know was that Sam had dug tanks underneath the floor of the winery. Then his pipefitter installed hidden valves and pipes on the backs of the tanks.

After the taxman left, they would open the secret valves and send that wine into the tanks under the floor. Then they would bring in *more grapes* to fill the upper tanks. This way Sam only paid half the tax, and by the time Prohibition was over, they had 600,000 gallons of wine aging under their floors. I'll bet the day after Prohibition was repealed Sam was sending that wine out in tanker cars to a thirsty country.

For an interesting insight into the United States alcohol laws, this taxation system still exists in the perfume industry. A cosmetics company will have a tank of alcohol on site, and each day they will pull a certain amount out and mix it with flower oils and other ingredients to create their perfumes. At the end of the day, they calculate the tax on the alcohol they've used and put a check in the mail to the alcohol tax bureau.

The wine and spirits industry still works under the shadow of *restrictive* laws carried over from the Prohibition era. That's why most American wineries don't have distilleries onsite, as is common in Europe, where they can hydrate their left-over pomace to make low cost, high-alcohol beverages like French marc, Italian grappa, Spanish orujo and Portuguese bagaço.

Unfortunately, not every California winery had such an inventive and painless solution to Prohibition. In Northern Sonoma, on the edge of the town of Healdsburg, the Simi Winery, started by two Italian friends, had done very well for many years, buying land and building a large winery. Both partners passed away and one of their daughters was left to guard their legacy.

When Prohibition began, the feeling among many of the Italian winemakers, for whom wine was in their blood, was that this was an impossible law and that it couldn't last. Italian culture by its very nature is *patient*, so many people felt they could wait it out until these foolish people in Washington DC came to their senses.

The daughter wasn't willing to risk Sam's strategy, and selling grapes alone was not bringing in enough revenue to sustain them, so over the course of the thirteen years she sold pieces of land to pay the taxes and cover the expenses required to keep the winery whole. By the time Prohibition was over, their operation was much smaller, but they had endured, and they were still on their feet! The winery has changed hands over the years, but you can visit it and taste their wines when you travel to Healdsburg in Northern Sonoma.

An often-told story in southern Napa is about the black chickens of the Biale Family Winery. This is not a Prohibition story, but instead about how the locals felt about the government taxing something as divinely essential as wine. In the early days of telephone service, those spread-out farmhouses were connected by 'party lines.' When you were on the phone, your neighbors could pick up their phone and hear your conversation. It provided a great deal of entertainment, like today's social media, for bored farm wives and children who spent too much time cut off from their neighbors. You knew that if you had any secrets, you shouldn't talk about them on the phone because they wouldn't be secrets for long.

For the Italians wine is food, so they didn't understand why it should be taxed any differently from carrots? Luckily, Napa and Sonoma, before and after Prohibition, were filled with what today we call artisan winemakers. These are small family affairs that have passed down the skills for generations. So, if you wanted to buy some wine without having to pay those pesky taxes, you could find someone to sell it to you. But one of the problems with a small wine producer is that *they run out of wine.* So, the best thing to do before you hopped in your truck and headed over the rough country roads was to call them up on the phone and see if they had any wine left. How do you ask them about that when your neighbors could be listening in on your conversation?

The answer to that requires a little history. The Biale family, whose farm and winery are on Big Ranch Road in Napa's Oak Knoll District, in the southeastern part of the valley, grew kitchen vegetables that they sold at the local market. As is common with a small farm, they also raised chickens. This home business supplemented what the father earned as a miner in the distant mountains. But then he died in a mining accident, leaving the family in desperate straits. The oldest son, who was only twelve years old, announced to his mother that he would make wine for sale, and he did. When they drove their wagon full of vegetables to the markets, they hid the bottles of tax-free wine under the produce.

As his wine got better, Biale became known as one of the places to buy good wine tax free. But that was illegal, so they developed a code. When their neighbors called on the party line looking for wine, they knew to ask, "Do you have any *black chickens* for sale?" If they said 'yes,' they could head on over and buy a couple of bottles. Biale eventually became a legal, bonded winery, as did their neighbors, the Regusci family, located just a couple of miles north of the Biale's winery on the Silverado Trail.

At one time the 'Trail' passed right in front of the Regusci's big stone barn, built by Captain John Grigsby in the late 1800s. Today the Trail travels further to the west on a more level part of the valley floor. During Prohibition, Grandpa Regusci had his own home-based solution to the 'crazy law.' He built a still in a side room in the barn and brewed bottles of 'hooch' for sale. Whenever he had some ready, he would leave a lamp on in the little peak window at the top of the barn where people driving by could see it shining from a distance.

The reality was, Prohibition was *disastrous* for the overall health of the nation. Before it was enacted most of the country was drinking healthy, low alcohol beverages like wine, beer and hard cider. In the cities those were often preferred to the water coming out of the taps, which was not always as safe to drink. Before Prohibition, most apples went into cider and they were only popularized to eat as raw fruit, in pies and as apple sauce when the hard cider businesses were shut down.

The reasons for Prohibition had less to do with alcohol and more to do with society's propensity for war. At the end of the Civil War, during which a bizarre number of American soldiers were killed and wounded, the main tool that veterans had for dealing with post-traumatic stress was alcohol. Hard liquor was more common in the cities and after returning from the war, husbands, fathers and sons by the thousands disappeared into bars.

It was a blight that left families destitute. That was when the 'Temperance' movement started, but then there was the Spanish American War, during which most of the fatalities were due to tropical diseases. Then sixteen years later came the incredibly brutal trench warfare of World War One. When the Temperance crusaders saw veterans coming home after that trauma, and heading for the bars, those childhood memories of the years after the Civil War were surprisingly fresh. Women especially knew what was going to come next and it gave them the impetus to push the eighteenth amendment through in 1919. To give you a time marker, women got the right to vote with the nineteenth amendment in 1920.

The problem was, wine and beer has been part of human nutrition for *millennia* for good reasons, people like to drink it, it makes them feel better, removes their aches and provides some significant health benefits. Hard alcohol was a more recent arrival in Europe, and this was not the first disaster it had created. But because wine required more time to make and was bulky to transport, the very profitable, illicit bootlegging business shifted towards making and smuggling hard liquor. For people who understood the basics of fermentation it was simple to make. All you needed was a pile of corn or grain, some water and yeast, and a small still you could build yourself.

You could make a variety of high proof liquors in a *fraction* of the time required to make wine and pour it into smaller bottles that were easier to hide and transport than those big wine jugs. During Prohibition, the east side of the city of Napa, where the Italians lived, was a hidden forest of stills. Every now and then people would hear explosions from that neighborhood, followed by the bell of the fire trucks.

They knew that the swirly copper tube on the top of someone's still had clogged up and the tank had dramatically burst its seams. It was estimated that New York City had as many as a *hundred thousand* speakeasies and tens of thousands of illegal stills supplying them. Even after prohibition in the United States, there continues to be plenty of clandestine stills producing tax free liquor.

As you drive up the Napa Valley these days, just as you pass the 'Welcome to Napa Valley' sign on the left, you can see the Far Niente winery sitting beyond it, surrounded by its vineyards. During Prohibition it was owned by a wealthy woman who had been widowed, and married a younger, handsome, and quite dashing WWI flying ace. Someplace in that big winery there was a still, because the Ace built an airstrip, so he could make deliveries with his plane.

As time went on and he got busier and busier, he added two more strips so he could always take off into the wind. Unfortunately, his stepdaughter hated this enterprising pilot and poisoned him. Eventually, family dysfunction and Prohibition got the better of them and the building was boarded up and silent for almost sixty years, Finally, the Nickel family revived the property and dug the first *new caves* in Napa in the 20th century.

As the country abandoned wine, beer and cider in favor of hard liquor, liver disease and alcoholism sky-rocketed. This campaign by the 'sobriety crusaders' had produced horrible, unintended consequences, damaging the society they were trying to help. It also produced fortunes for bootleggers and the rise of the criminal class.

One legal remnant of those thirteen years is a pile of regulations related to alcohol production that requires wineries to have compliance officers to keep the paperwork current. Another remnant is a bizarrely convoluted alcohol distribution system, which was set up after Prohibition by Meyer Lansky, the Mob's accountant. For many years, if a company wanted to have their wine or liquor distributed in a city, they would have to bring an envelope of cash to grease the wheels with the distributor.

The third remnant of Prohibition was effectively a ban on home beermaking that persisted until the Carter administration. While home winemaking continued through Prohibition, thanks to its connections with the Bible, beermaking was completely shut down. However, the regulations related to beer were so draconic that even after Prohibition was repealed, only the largest companies could handle all the requirements to have a brewery. Why was Congress *so hard* on the beermakers?

Because Prohibition became law in 1919, right after the First World War when the lawmakers were still mad at the German American families who owned many of the breweries. But then, during the Carter administration, the regulations were relaxed and home beermaking became legal again.

That was when we saw the growth of the Micro-Brewery, especially in Sonoma. Why? Because winemakers are traditionally beer drinkers! After an entire day of working with wine, that's the last thing they want to drink. Instead, they prefer to relax with a nice, cold glass of beer. Sonoma also had a long tradition of growing superior hops, and these Sonoma winemakers had all the equipment necessary to make their own beer, and so they did. After a while they got good at it, and the artisan brewery was born.

During Prohibition, while the large Italian population in Sonoma expanded their vineyards, the growers in Napa went in a different direction. In Napa, where there was a larger percentage of Americans, Prussians and French vintners, they were concerned with being seen as disreputable, because they were producing grapes that could be made into wine.

Their main profits came from winemaking, so south of Saint Helena, farmers ripped out vineyards and planted fruit and nut trees or brought in cattle or sheep to graze. Today there are still sections of both counties devoted to cattle, sheep, goats and horses. In the northern part of the valley there was a large population of Italian American growers. Many had arrived looking for work as masons and laborers. Growing grapes was in their blood, so they kept their Zinfandel vineyards, shipping their grapes to the East Coast in box cars filled with dry ice.

However, there were so many people who understood fermentation, that the speakeasies of Napa became
a favorite destination for folks from the city seeking a
fun time. Those unlit, winding country roads, filled with
drunk drivers, were littered with crashes. The shame of
Prohibition is that Napa and Sonoma's hundreds of wineries had been producing an abundance of healthy wines,
and thanks to this short-sighted, misguided policy, it
would be forty years before a new crop of wineries would
blossom in those beautiful valleys.

Above: Regusci WInery
Opposite: Robledo Winery

Chapter Seventeen
The Mexican Influence

In the 1960's and 1970's, when new money started coming into the North Bay Wine Country, there were almost no Mexican families living there. That should seem odd since this region was *part of Spain,* and then Mexico, for longer than it's been part of the United States. Even though growing wine grapes has been an occupation here for generations, since the end of Prohibition, the work was done by farmers sitting on their tractors. They planted vines wide enough that there was plenty of room between the rows for their *'John Deere.'*

The only time Mexican workers came here was to pick the fruit, whether it was plums, walnuts or wine grapes. In those days, the grapes that the locals grew mostly went into what the industry calls jug wines, inexpensive vintages made in big commercial wineries and sold in large bottles under a variety of labels.

Then in the 1970's that model began to change. We'd like to think that was due to the famed "Judgment of Paris" tasting, which showed off the California wines in such a spectacular way. Many believe that it kicked off the renaissance, but there were many other factors that transformed this region from a producer of jug wines to a premium wine destination. If the growing conditions are equal, the main difference between an inexpensive wine, and a price tag that makes you *catch your breath*, is the number of times that workers go into the vineyard to tend the plants.

Yes, there are factors in location and microclimates that determine whether a vineyard has the potential to produce wonderful grapes, and yes, the North Bay is one of the best places. But, once that is recognized and the owner commits to planting the vines, the difference comes down to how many times someone looks at each vine and does what needs to be done. For a vineyard owner, every time a team goes between the vines, it *costs them money*. After that, any difference in quality comes down to how much fruit they are willing to reject to make sure only the best goes into their bottles and how well the weather supports their work.

But *it all starts* in the vineyard, which is a field of berry bushes. Once they're planted, they'll start producing fruit after about three years. Then they'll continue producing grapes for twenty, thirty, forty or more years, depending on the grape variety and the vagaries of the market and disease. A grower of grapes for bulk wines will send machinery into the vineyard five times a year. A premium producer might send teams of workers into the vineyard *ten, or even twenty times* a year, often with hand tools for pruning, grafting and picking. For large scale work, a small vineyard might turn to a management company, but they'll have one or two workers who are continually doing this and that to keep the vines happy. Only the largest vineyards typically have a full-time team capable of doing all the work.

In the North Bay wine region, the typical vineyard is ten to twenty acres. A large vineyard of five hundred acres will require about twenty workers. To put this in perspective, in the central valley where the bulk wine grapes are grown today, *entirely* using machinery, a 20-acre vineyard would be a hobby farm. But the premium growers in the North Bay can earn five or ten times more per ton for their grapes than in the Central Valley, because of much better growing conditions, although with smaller yields.

It's hard to beat the North Bay's weather. It alternates between hot, dry, incredibly bright days in the ideal eighty-degree range, followed by cool, foggy nights that preserve the acid in the grapes, and provide the vines with just the right amount of water. As it became obvious that great grapes could be grown here, vineyard owners started looking for full time workers who had the necessary skills. As a result, the North Bay vineyard teams are among the *highest* paid agricultural workers in the country.

As more wineries began turning out premium wines, the demand for full-time workers grew. Those young Mexican men who came here to pick grapes during harvest time, started finding full time positions at the vineyards, and made this their home. Well, young men with good jobs attract young women, and so their girlfriends and wives came north from Mexico.

Then their babies were born here in Northern California and grew up speaking English and Spanish and translating for their parents. As the grapes began earning more per ton, the workers' skills became more valuable to the growers, along with their need to hold onto folks who would develop a relationship with the vineyards that they tended year after year.

Working in the vineyards is hard and the vines are often low to the ground, requiring a great deal of bending. It requires a hearty constitution and bodies accustomed to agricultural work. Fortunately, the Mexican workers tended to be compact and tough, making them suited to tending the vines.

But it is not about brute strength. When it comes to the pruning, the *crews of women* are among the highest paid, because their dexterity is critical to attaining superior results. The way they prune the vines affects the next two years of production and there is *no undo button* once the canes fall to the ground. As wineries became more successful, they added more full-time workers, and when vineyards changed hands the workers familiar with that land normally stayed on. There are world renowned vineyards in the North Bay that have been cared for by three generations of the same family, originally from Mexico.

Convincing vines to produce superior fruit is a demanding process, and the workers are diligently trained. They often come up through a familial mentoring system when nieces and nephews get jobs thanks to an uncle or aunt's recommendation. That means that they have the dual pressure of being under the eyes of both their boss and their Tio or Tia, who knows that this kid's performance reflects on them. Many of the workers we see in the vineyards send a large part of their weekly pay home to Mexico.

The vineyard manager or consultant develops the strategy that the team then implements, and learning all the steps and techniques required in their work takes time. In the springtime, soon after the first leaves appear, they sucker the vines, trimming away any leaves on the long woody stock. That both promotes more vigorous growth on the canopy above and limits the potential of insects climbing up the vine from the ground. As the new canes spring out, workers will walk between the vines and weave the flexible wood into the wires above.

That way the vine can take full advantage of the sunshine while limiting the amount of shade that falls on the developing grapes below. As the vines fill out, workers may trim away any leaves shading the thick-skinned grapes like Cabernet Sauvignon or leave them in place if they need to protect the delicate, thin skin varieties, like Pinot Noir, from the hot sun. You'll see *both men and women* out between the vines soon after dawn, and they'll often spend most of the day working in the bright, hot sun. Fortunately, California is a place that values its workers, so due to state regulations, when it's over ninety degrees, work stops in the vineyards. They pitch tents in the vineyard provide shade for breaks, and insulated jugs of icy water to keep them hydrated.

At harvest time you can always tell when the pickers have moved through the vines by the line of leaves on the ground, and the yellowing leaves around where the grapes had been hanging. You can practically see the plants relax as they are relieved of their load, and soon after, the green leaves will turn golden yellow.

In the *wintertime rainy season,* the winds will shake the leaves off the vines and work will stop in the vineyards. This is when the workers customarily visit their families in Mexico for the Christmas holiday. But after the New Year they'll return because there's work that needs to be done, pruning away last year's canes and preparing the vines for the coming season.

In recent years, the demand for workers has grown so high that as soon as the leaves are off the vines from the first blustery wintertime rains, lines of workers cars will appear alongside the vineyards, as the teams head in between the vines with their tools in hand.

But those wintertime rains can bring work to a halt because the tractors running through the mud can tear up carefully groomed rows, and trimming vines when they are wet makes them vulnerable to fungus. If conditions merit, the workers paint the cut tips with a gray green fungicide to forestall any problems. As the winter stretches on, we watch patches of vineyards, here and there trimmed back to the sturdy wood. And in the Springtime, there will always be the odd vineyard where last year's canes are still intact, with tiny green leaves sprouting along their willowy length. It makes you wonder, was the owner late paying last year's contractor bill, or did they forget to schedule a crew, or are they planning to rip out the vines, so they didn't bother with the pruning? Usually, it's the latter!

This region has suffered from a string of devasting fires, so many of the Mexican men found jobs in construction rebuilding burnt houses. Meanwhile others went to work for the now legal cannabis growers. As a result, it's become increasingly hard to find vineyard workers.

Fifty years after the Judgment of Paris, the children of that first generation aren't doing that work, because they went to the local colleges and the state's Universities, learning the art and science of wine.

They are the winery managers, winemakers, executives and owners. At Napa County College, with its world class wine production program, forty percent of the students are bilingual in English and Spanish. So, the region depends on new workers coming from Mexico.

It is fortunate that there are more workers on hand during harvest than at any other time because during the late summer fires of 2017, 2019 and 2020 they went back and forth from *picking grapes to fighting the fires*. It is helpful to understand that California farmers know how to fight fires and the same bulldozers, water trucks and shovels they use for developing vineyards, work just as well for cutting fire breaks and soaking hotspots.

The 2017 fire broke out at night in high winds, right in the middle of harvest. The first week, before the fire companies arrived with their helicopters and flying water tankers, the local police and fire companies were entirely involved with moving people out of the path of the flames. But, *from the first day,* the local ranchers and their teams split their time between picking the fruit and fighting the flames. It was their toughness and determination that prevented the fire from becoming a catastrophe.

Wine Country is always evolving, and the biggest change is in how the winery tasting rooms changed due to COVID. During that period the wineries, which are food producers, stayed open. They could see a limited number of appointments, hosted outside, often on brand new patio furniture. But the real transformation in the tasting rooms took place in the staff. Before the shutdown, *'Boomers'* made up about forty percent of the tasting room staff. In some tasting rooms it was more like one hundred percent gray hairs.

These were people who had retired from other jobs and wanted a part-time job to get them out of the house. It was fun, not very strenuous and the wineries loved them because they didn't demand much in pay, or benefits, and they were very patient with the customers, which is important in wine sales. But when COVID began it ravaged that generation and they were all sent home. Well, the thing about the Boomers is that they are very resourceful. They were raised by 'The Greatest Generation' who expected a lot from them. So, when they went home, they *found other things to do*; starting businesses, getting involved with their grandkids, or volunteering.

When the tasting rooms reopened, they called their former employees to come back, and only about one in ten Boomers returned. The wineries were in a jam. They had been paying peanuts for part-time workers when no appointments were required. Now every tasting was *by appointment, and more expensive,* and they needed dependable help. To get workers to apply, they doubled what they previously paid and offered full-time jobs with benefits and commissions.

Suddenly the young people who had grown up in this region, many with Mexican parents who worked in the industry, for the first time took a serious look at these jobs. They would never have touched them before, with their part-time hours and low pay. But now they saw the opportunity to work in the industry that was part of their family tradition for good pay. It also meant not having to travel outside the area to get a decent paying job. When they started their new positions, they saw that most of their co-workers were also young, which meant they were able to work with potential friends and partners.

This solved a major problem that the wineries had been struggling with for many years. The clientele in the tasting rooms was getting older, and they were buying less wine. They needed to attract younger customers who would develop a loyalty to the brand and buy their wines for many years to come. Suddenly they saw that having a younger team in the tasting room was attracting younger customers. Also, many of the new team members are *bilingual in English and Spanish, w*hich means they are attracting another sizable demographic, the Spanish speakers.

It turns out that all the wineries needed to do to solve their demographic challenge in the tasting room was to endure a major pandemic. Clearly this is a case where a box of lemons became a pitcher of tasty limoncello.

How is this going to change the future of wine country, as these young Mexican Americans become increasingly knowledgeable about the business of wine? It is inevitable that their customer sales experience and evolving opinions will shape the future of the region, which is only right sincethe Mexican traditions are so much a part of its past.

Chapter Eighteen
The Evolution of the Tasting Room

Today, in the North Bay Wine Country, there are so many tasting rooms that it's hard to imagine a time when you couldn't go there and have a drink. That unique enterprise is perfectly appropriate because the North Bay has a long tradition, dating back to the mid-1800's, of being the place where people found the best wines and brandies.

Even though Sonoma was the site of the first North Bay wineries, the oldest 'tasting room' that I know of was built for Napa's famous Inglenook Estate. *It's still there,* although preserved as an historical moment in time, rather than a place where you can taste the owner's best. When you look in through the Dutch door you see echoes of the past, and the owner's history, with his portrait. Gustave Niebaum was a ship's captain who had gone to sea as a young boy. Later in life he made his fortune transporting furs from the icy northwest to San Francisco.

Niebaum was the first winemaker in Napa to put his own brand name, Inglenook, on his wine bottles. The name refers to a small, cozy nook near a fireplace, an architectural feature that preceded central heating, where people would gather for warmth and company. The creation of his tasting room grew from a practical need to sample wines with his guests, someplace warmer than his cool, stone winery, especially in the winter.

So, inside the entrance he constructed a 'wooden box.' As a sailor, he had spent much of his life in timber cabins on wooden ships, and his tasting room harkens back to a *ship Captain's stateroom*. It comes complete with brackets to stop glasses and bottles from falling off the high shelves as the ship rolled with the waves, a helpful feature in earthquake country.

By his tasting room are two German quotes, auf Deutsch: *"Im Wein Liegt Wahrheit Nur Allein*, or *"In wine lies truth, only alone."* And another that looks to the future, auf Deutsch, *"Schenk Mir Ein, Einem Alten Wein, Dass Mein Herz Kann Frohlich Sein,"*
Or (not literally),

"Give me a glass of very old wine, so happy can be this heart of mine." With that, Gustave Niebaum formally planted the seed of tourism in Wine Country.

The 20th Century

At the beginning of the 20th Century, the North Bay wines were traveling on a good trajectory. They had survived the phylloxera epidemic and benefitted from the disruption of the French Wineries during WWI, which created opportunities for America's premium producers. But then in 1919, in response to the rampant alcoholism flaring up among returning veterans, Prohibition began.

For the next 13 years, North Bay tourism centered around the *mineral hot springs* in Sonoma and Napa. Interestingly, in the 1800's the two largest hotels in California were hot springs resorts in Napa. Many companies bottled and sold mineral waters and at one time there were dozens of local brands. Just north of the Sonoma Plaza, the towns of Aqua Caliente and Boyes Hot Springs were home to a delightful collection of spas including the still existent Sonoma Mission Inn.

Unfortunately, after the *1906 earthquake,* the springs in that area gradually *withdrew* into the earth. Today the Sonoma Mission Inn depends on wells for their mineral water. Their less resourceful neighbor spas closed. The springs in Northern Napa, being closer to Lake County's quasi-dormant volcanos, are still bubbling to the surface.

During Prohibition, the other popular North Bay 'tourism' were the local speakeasies and brothels. It was a hard business run by women, but the numerous distillers in the area guaranteed them a steady supply of liquor. On the downside, with so many inebriated drivers trying to find their way, those dark country roads suffered from an epidemic of car wrecks. Even today, the North Bay has twice the DUI rate of the rest of California. However, a fair amount of that can be blamed on folks who work in the industry and simply get used to being a little 'buzzed' all day long, and don't consider it when they go out on the road.

Weed in Wine Country

In many ways this underground enterprise was repeated years later, thanks to the federal prohibition on cannabis, that started a few years after alcohol Prohibition ended. This was political maneuver by the director of the Federal Bureau of Narcotics to find a new mission for his agency, now that alcohol was legal. It also gave law enforcement a legal tool to control the Mexicans, for whom this was a popular intoxicant.

Illegal cannabis farming and distribution became a major financial contributor in three of the rural counties north of Sonoma and Napa. Before California decriminalized cannabis for recreational uses, having neighbors in the trade came with pluses and minuses. It was nice that your property values increased, but on the other hand, your neighbors all carried guns, and an awful lot of people looked stoned half the time.

For many years in what is known as the Emerald Triangle, growing illegal 'weed' was a bigger part of local economies than logging. Sonoma also did its share of growing, but being more heavily populated, the 'farms' were typically inside warehouses with grow lights, or in between rows of grapevines. Quite a few vineyard managers had sidelines setting up '*grows*' for their clients.

There's an excellent vineyard on the hills overlooking downtown Sonoma that was originally intended as a cannabis grow, but then the consultant told the owner that it would make a better vineyard, so they grow grapes instead. Napa is such a small county, and so carefully managed, that any illicit plot was typically found so quickly that it wasn't worth the investment. Once growing recreational cannabis was made legal, many counties, including Sonoma, were open to the plans of ambitious farmers.

However, Napa has been resistant to '*weed,*' and of course most people will think that's because they don't want it competing with the wine. Actually, it's because they don't want cannabis plots competing with the vines for the *available water*. Napa is much drier than Sonoma, getting about half the annual rainfall. Farmers in Napa carefully guard their water supplies in retention ponds, and there are years when they go dry.

An acre of grapes, at the most, will use ninety thousand gallons of water annually, and some dry farm the vines, so they only use a little when planting new vines. In Sonoma, cannabis plots are restricted in size, but they need a *million* gallons of water per acre each year. That's enough water for ten acres of vines, which is the average size of a Napa vineyard. But that's enough for now about the all too long federal cannabis prohibition, so let's go back to the equally nonsensical prohibition of wine.

Eventually alcohol restrictions did about as much damage as it could manage and the country said, 'enough.' In the years running up to Prohibition, the winemakers had consistently touted the healthfulness of their products, with good reason. Wine is an antiseptic, potable, relaxing, antioxidant rich, tasty beverage. It can be made sweet or dry, and long before carrot juice smoothies and kale shakes, wine was the original health drink. The idea of a place that has health spas and abundant amounts of good tasting wine sounds irresistible. But now the few wineries left in the North Bay were struggling to fill the demand for the newly legal products, so tasting rooms were *superfluous*. Wineries could sell their products sight unseen, or untasted by the tanker full, but over time wine tourism gradually returned.

One of the true leaders in this tourism revival was the general manager at the Beringer Brothers Winery in the town of Saint Helena. He circulated flyers about the winery at the 1939 Golden Gate International Exposition, held on the newly created Treasure Island in San Francisco Bay, at the feet of the newly opened Bay Bridge. He *courted celebrities,* newspapers and magazines to get photo essays showing the gorgeous region, with glamorous couples sipping wine in the cellar. Beringer offered tours of the winery and cave that always ended with a tasting and, of course sales because wine is one of the world's best souvenirs!

In Northern Sonoma, the Italian Swiss Colony Winery, which had also started in the late 1800's, constructed a *replica* of a Northern Italian-Swiss mountain village. Families could spend the day there, enjoying food and wine, with picnic grounds and entertainments far from the city. Even though this was a two-hour drive north from San Francisco, in the 1960's it was second only to Disneyland as California's most popular tourist destination.

Napa in the 1960's

When Robert Mondavi bought the land for his eponymous winery, he chose the site for the great vineyard location, known as To Kalon, or the 'most high,' because this part of the valley floor rises up. Mondavi had gone to school at Stanford for marketing, so being in the heart of the valley made sense. When the architect came to see the property, he suggested putting the winery up against the hills so they could have caves connected to the back.

This was the way that Inglenook, Far Niente and Beringer were designed. But the hills are quite a distance from the road and Bob Mondavi told him, *"No, we've got to be right on the road where people can see us, because I don't have an advertising budget."* In terms of tourism, his new winery was on the wrong, aka, left side of the road.

At that time there were no center turn lanes on Highway 29, so when people drove north it was much easier for them to turn right into the wineries of B.V. or Louis M. Martini. So, Bob Mondavi sent people out to the front gate with signs saying, *'Free Winery Tour and*

Tasting' to wave people in. The tour was a big draw for a winery that was still small.

When the grapes were coming in during harvest, the tour included walking through puddles and jumping over hoses. People *loved* the experience, and ever since then, Mondavi has had one the valley's most sophisticated hospitality programs. Half of their team is devoted to hospitality while the other half makes and markets the wine!

By the 1970's there were about twenty wineries in the Napa Valley and about twice that many in larger Sonoma, but with these few exceptions, many didn't have formal tasting rooms. If they had anything, it was just an old door, spanning a pair of upended barrels to serve as a bar. Even in the early 2000's the revered Stag's Leap Cellars poured their wines in a *poorly lit* tank room, with one rough bar for the standard tasting, and another for the reserve. The fellows who poured for you could have just as soon worked in a hardware store, for the amount they told you about the wine, or its history.

It wasn't until they changed hands in 2007 that the new owners began building a separate hospitality space. The building had been designed years before, as part of the Stag's Leap caves, but while the caves were dug, the hospitality building was left for later. Well, 2007 was sufficiently *'later'* and today the guests enjoy wonderful views of the vineyards and the hillsides beyond.

Of course, there was also a practical reason for that decision. It's helpful to understand that in the wine business they have their priorities based on the process.

The money and space for grape growing always comes first, winemaking comes second, and hospitality, like the youngest, almost forgotten child, comes last. The tasting room teams are expected to make do with less and still be happy about it.

The room where Stag's Leap had been hosting their guests for years was a tank room, zoned for winemaking. Well, the new owners wanted to expand production of that specific wine, which required placing more tanks in that room so the hospitality folks needed to move, fortunately, to a much nicer space.

It's helpful to understand that many winery owners are primarily focused on the vineyards and the grapes. The saying that the wine is made in the vineyard is true, the actions they take there will affect the quality of the wine for years to come. For many owners hospitality was always an *afterthought*.

Usually, the turning point was when they hired a smart and bossy hospitality director, who shamed them into investing money in that part of the business where sales happen. As tour guides, that's the part of the winery we see the most, and the way the tasting room is designed and managed, makes a profound difference when it comes to the guest's experience and of course, wine sales.

Because the Napa Valley is only thirty miles long, which is *compact* compared to spread out Sonoma, the vintners are close together, forming a cozy collection of convenient tasting rooms. In the years before the new millennium, college students and families would drive up on the weekends to enjoy a very inexpensive, inebriated day in the country. The wines of Robert Mondavi, Beaulieu Vineyards, Louis M. Martini, Charles Krug, Christian Brothers, Beringer and Inglenook could be tasted for free just by dropping by.

Not surprisingly, the Napa Valley earned the nickname, *"The world's largest free bar."* Admittedly, the tastings were free because the wines were so cheap. The best bottle at Stag's Leap in 1976 was six dollars. This was before the days of fine, hand tended agriculture. Everything was done from the seat of a tractor and the only time the Mexican pickers came into the area was during the harvest.

Most of the larger wineries were distributed through retail stores, so having a local tasting room on-site was considered part of their marketing plan. Small wineries found that if they put up an *'open' sign* and kept clean glasses handy, they could sell plenty of their wine, at retail prices. While there are regulations, they treat wineries a little more like a farm stand offering samples, and less like a bar selling hard liquor.

Some vintners started off pouring wine for folks on their back porch. Eventually they developed favorite customers, which led to wine clubs and parties, where folks could come together for wine, food and music. After the guests left their spouse would say, *"Do you realize how much wine we sold?"* They didn't, but by the next week they had a new wine cooler in the tank room and a heater under that table, and they were off to the races.

In the same way that winemaking is by its nature, a long-term project, the way families developed their hospitality was also slow and incremental. What started off as a rustic tasting room eventually becomes homey. Then as more artifacts from their history accumulate, they become fun and filled with personality. If the property is sold to a corporate team, they may save a bit of that history to promote the brand, but often the space becomes slick and stylish. Over eighty percent of the North Bay wineries are small family affairs.

Most visitors to wine country taste in comfortably designed hospitality spaces with easily cleaned surfaces which stand up to spilled wine. But there are still plenty of small family wineries that are off the beaten path, that host guests in their tank rooms or back porches. At the smallest wineries, the host will be the winemaker, or a family member. When a winery produces over a certain number of annual cases, or the bottles are sufficiently expensive, the host will be a professional, even though it may take place in a private home.

Sometimes when a well-run winery changes hands you can't tell because the new owner figures that the system is working well so don't mess with success. But sometimes an owner will put their stamp on the new property and a perfect example is Jess Jackson, the owner of Kendall-Jackson. Over the years he bought a shocking number of small, high-quality wineries. While the wines stayed the same, the tasting rooms all started to look like high-end law offices, which was Jess's original profession. He felt that what worked for one should work for all! That would not be my preferred approach, but at least he paid attention to the *hospitality.*

Gradually the number of *destination* wineries has increased. These are places where the architecture, the interiors and the views, afford great photo opportunities, which are reasons enough to visit. They are exciting, although they can so overwhelm the senses, that the wine tasting seems secondary. When the building features a brand that's widely distributed, a dramatic hospitality center is an important part of their advertising. When people visit the winery, they're more inclined to order it on a restaurant's wine list or pick up a bottle at their local wine shop. Think of brands like Ferrari Carano, Chateau St. Jean, Domaine Carneros, Artesa and of course, Robert Mondavi.

During 2020 and 2021, when so many businesses and restaurants were closed, the wineries were permitted *to stay open* because they're food producers. Since a big part of modern winemaking is founded on serious science, there was never a question about whether they were going to take measures to keep their teams and their guests healthy. Across the North Bay, wineries *expanded their patios,* and purchased new outdoor furniture, heaters and tents to keep the occasional rain off. Luckily, their guests adapted to the outdoor tastings very quickly, happy to be closer to nature and doing something social that included wine.

The old tasting bars mostly disappeared, and we don't expect many to return in the near future. Instead, guests who were accustomed to dropping in, now need appointments at most wineries. They are seated at comfortably spaced tables where the overall feeling is more relaxed and gracious than the chaos of the old tasting rooms. When the winery management realized that the new model was producing more sales with fewer customers, they quickly abandoned the old 'drop by and stand at the bar' model.

Most modern people spend their lives feeling separated from nature. Coming to the wineries infuses their souls with that fundamental connection to nature that they can see, smell and taste. That's one of the reasons that the wine clubs are so popular. Every time new bottles show up at their home, it brings them back to that place with those wonderful flavors and *good feelings* that made them feel happy and welcome.

Tasting Room at Raymond Winery

Chateau Saint Jean Winery

Chapter Nineteen
Why Wine Moves Us

I would often suggest to my clients that after **a** day of visiting wineries, they should plan to have a simple dinner at, or near, the hotel right after the tour. That's because a day on the road that includes three wineries, where each pours the equivalent of a glass or two of wine, can be exhausting. But the effect is not due solely to the considerable amount of alcohol they've consumed.

If a person drinks enough water during the tour, it *spreads* the effects of the alcohol throughout the body, so that even their feet feel good, and their head just feels light. Back in the 1920's people described that feeling as being 'lit', and in ancient times they talked about feeling 'illuminated' by the wine. On the day of the tour, when a person eats breakfast and lunch that's mostly protein and fat, while avoiding excessive carbohydrates, they improve what we call their tasting endurance. That's how long they can go without feeling loopy! Alcohol and acid from the wine get tied up in releasing the *energy* trapped in those foods, while coincidentally reducing the inebriating effects of the wine.

When a person follows these simple strategies, they can avoid dehydration and erratic shifts in their blood sugar, so their body will tolerate, and in fact enjoy, an impressive amount of wine. I've had clients who have taken these steps to heart so completely that they later complained, after a tasting or two, that they weren't getting enough of a buzz. I reminded them that this was a wine tasting, not a wine drinking. We want them to remember where they went!

In this strategy there is a caveat related to cheese, something that seems like a natural companion to wine. I remember a client who responded to my suggestion about eating protein by having a huge amount of cheese for lunch. While that sounded like a promising idea, because cheeses can be as high as 40% carbohydrates, her blood sugar spiked and then dropped like a rock, so after that nice lunch she fell asleep in the car. Always adaptable, we dropped her off at the hotel and her husband and I continued visiting wineries.

Excessive alcohol, dehydration and plummeting blood sugar are the usual reasons people get tired after a wine tour, so we couldn't blame her for punking out. That combination of sugar and fat is irresistible, even though it is rarely found in nature. In contrast, it's prevalent in many popular foods like ice cream. Why do we find it so easy to overeat foods with that combination of nutrients? Because the *one food in nature* where we do encounter this pairing is in mother's milk! The design of the human palate is programed to encourage us to consume this combination to the edge of excess, because babies need to put on weight quickly. The high sugar turns on the insulin that tells the body to store, rather than burn the fat as fuel.

That's why a chubby baby is the quintessential definition of 'cute.' That unique program that makes people crave cheese and ice cream, doesn't turn off as we age, and junk food manufacturers have made fortunes thanks to that reality. So, when you're at a wine tasting, don't overdo the cheese please!

One of the reasons why wine tastings are special experiences is due to the deep power that scent and flavor have over our emotions and our sense of place. Ask yourself this, how often have you tasted something and felt *transported* to somewhere you hadn't visited for years? It is something that most people experience! Did one of your siblings ever make one of your mom's favorite recipes, for example chicken soup, but they changed an ingredient? *How long did it take you to notice?* What's the speed of light? How did it make you feel? What was the expression on your face when you called them on it? It spoke volumes from the emotional depths of your soul!

Have you ever tasted a wine and recognized that specific grape's flavor, triggering a strong emotional reaction and yet, leaving you baffled about where you tasted it previously? That happened to me at a tasting room in downtown Napa, with a Vermentino from the Los Carneros District. Suddenly I smelled the ocean and it 'felt' like Italy to me, all sunny and relaxed. It took an extensive web search to discover that I had first drunk quite a bit of Vermentino, twenty years before, while carving marble on the coast of the southern Italian Riviera. No wonder I found those flavors so appealing!

Every one of these very emotional experiences started when a particle of wine, food or a flower touched the inside of your nose, or your taste buds. While the senses of sight and hearing are interpreted by the frontal part of the brain, your sense of scent and flavor live in the ancient parts where *emotions* and *spatial awareness* reside.

That part of the brain is also where speech lives. Consider, have you ever inhaled the scent of an exotic perfume on a lovely neck and found yourself speechless? Have you ever tasted something so good that it was beyond description? That's because scents, and to a greater extent, flavors can take up so much *bandwidth* in that part of the brain, that there is no room left for speech to function. It's believed that there are only six major flavors: Salt, sweet, bitter, umami, spice, and sour, *but I don't think that's true.*

I do think that it's hard for us to describe them. The only way to truly communicate a flavor to someone else is to pour them the wine, or hand then a dish and give them a taste. That's why the most common way of describing a flavor is to say that "It tastes like...!"

In a true sense, flavor is its own language.

That's why chefs, winemakers and perfumers are revered in our culture. They create combinations of scents and flavors that take us on emotional journeys. In wine country, the winemakers are considered wizards because their job is to manage the complex of potential flavors from one fruit, the grape, into an appealing beverage.

They do have an advantage, because grapevines have an exceptionally complex genetic code compared to many fruits and vegetables. That allows them to adapt to changing environments and produce unique combinations of scents and flavors.

As a result, if you grow a grapevine on one side of a valley, you will get one collection of flavors. But, if you take a cutting from that vine, and plant it on the other side of the valley, due to the differences in geology, the soil's microflora, sunlight and wind patterns, they'll produce a different pattern of flavors.

Grapes grow all over the world in widely different climates and thanks to that mutable code, those diverse varieties can produce over a *thousand flavors*. Compare that to coffee beans, one of our favorite drinks, which produce about five hundred flavors, which is still impressive. Consider this, *if there are only six flavors, why do we all have favorite coffee beans?* In the grape, the diversity of flavors is due to their ability to adapt to so many climates and conditions, just like people do.

If all the plants on the Earth were animals, the grapevines would be the humans.

Because people enjoy wine and have a long history with the grapevine over many generations, growers have affected the evolution of the wine by selecting the vines that they wanted in their vineyard. They recognized that while the female plants produced substantial amounts of fruit, the male plants produced none, but you needed them around to produce pollen for the females. But they also realized that there was a third sex called a hermaphrodite, something that is *common* in the plant world as a species survival system. A hermaphrodite has both male and female organs, so they don't require male plants and bees to pollinate the vines. If there is a breeze in the vineyard the pollen will find the flowers. They also only produce half the fruit as the females.

Since all the nutrition of the plant goes into less fruit, it is more flavorful, which is highly desirable in wine grapes. Among premium growers, if the vines are producing too much fruit, they do what is called a green harvest. After *veraison*, when the grapes turn from green to their final color, they will cut off excess fruit and drop it on the ground, so more energy goes into the remaining bunches.

Today, all the vines you see in the vineyards are hermaphrodites. To maintain that requires propagating the plants from cuttings. Traditionally, farmers sowed seeds that they gathered from the previous year's best plants, although conventional grain farmers have abandoned that practice with the advent of chemical agriculture. But, if the grape growers used the seeds to propagate new vines every twenty or thirty years, even those from the hermaphrodites, they would produce males and females again. So, all the vines in a vineyard come from the same cuttings making them *genetically identical*. That eliminates the evolution that takes place through the seeds. Instead, growers have selectively propagated mutations that exhibited beneficial qualities, like a unique flavor, or being drought or disease resistant. Those mutations are called clones.

One of the ways in which wine is important in society is through offering a sense of continuity. The wines that the ancient Romans drank were almost identical to today's Pinot Noir and Syrah. There are very few agricultural pursuits that require quite the patience of grape growing and winemaking, so it often stays within families and organizations for generations.

Historically in Europe winemaking was the province of the nobility and the church, both conservative organizations. Because winemakers steadfastly cling to their past, the wines you drink today are genetically and culturally connected to the wines that your ancestors drank two thousand years ago.

This is the long way around to explaining why wine tasting at the vineyards can be so exhausting. It connects to our history through the ancient parts of the brain. The senses of sight and hearing sit high on the skull, and reach the brain through the frontal cortex, the domain of the conscious mind. There, the information is interpreted to make sense of the raw signals. Because the conscious mind remembers what it saw before, we approach the world with a host of convenient, visual preconceptions. That's why a magician's sleight-of-hand can be so effective. When your eyes see something different from what your brain expects to see, you have fooled yourself.

In contrast, the senses of smell and taste come through the *ancient* parts of the brain where emotions and speech live, so they are not interpreted for you by the brain the way sights and sounds are, so you will never forget them. When you are smelling and tasting a wide variety of scents and flavors with friends and family, you are triggering and sharing an array of emotions and memories.

During a holiday, when you are enjoying the traditional dishes that you grew up with, those recipes and feelings are being passed between the generations. Enjoying that meal with a wonderful bottle of wine is like being in an emotional waterfall, where the words you might use to describe it pale in comparison to the pleasant, sensual experiences that move through you.

While that kind of emotional journey can be exhausting enough, there is another factor to consider. Day in and day out you *ask little* of your nose and palate. You get up every day and start off with the same cup of coffee or tea, followed by a bite of a carbohydrate or protein to get you started. If you eat lunch out, you have a small list of items on the menu that you like. Even eating at home, your grocery list, week to week, is mostly the same items.

So, your nose and palate don't often encounter surprises. Even when people go out to dinner in Wine Country, they'll eat what they eat at home, simply more elegantly prepared, pricier and with no clean up. But when it comes to the wines during a day of tastings, you are on a sensory adventure.

A remarkable study funded by the Rockefeller Foundation revealed that *the nose can detect almost one billion scents.* Amazing, yes? Unfortunately, over ninety percent of those scents would be considered unpleasant. Many people can recognize an impressive eight hundred to twelve hundred distinct scents. They may not be able to name them, but they recognize them. A perfumer, because they work with scents all the time, may recognize and identify about two thousand. A winemaker will recognize an array of scents specific to wines and the winemaking process.

During fermentation, a good winemaker can tell how it is doing, and what else the yeast might need to be productive, by the scent and the sound of the escaping carbon dioxide bubbles.

The reason that the scents associated with wine are pleasant to our nose is because the nutrients it contains are beneficial to the body. So, your nervous system recognizes them as friends. During a wine tasting, having to use your senses of scent and taste in such a completely different, outside the box way can be exhausting, especially if it includes a food pairing. It's like doing intense physical work that you haven't done in a long time, the next day your muscles are sore. It's also like traveling to see family and close personal friends that you haven't seen in a while, by the time you get back home you feel like you *need a vacation from the vacation*. But in the case of wine tasting, the exhaustion is in the parts of the brain where your emotions live.

Winetasting for professionals is a different experience, because they've encountered those flavors so many times, that the emotional journeys they take them on are familiar. Imagine watching a movie you've seen many times. They know what emotions it is going to trigger, and they are able to move through them quickly. Having that previous experience allows a professional to focus on the wine, the color, the flavors and the mouth feel.

They also typically spit the wine out,
because otherwise,
after two or three sips
it all tastes good.

A joy for them is tasting a great wine that is completely outside of their previous experience. It's like taking a trip to somewhere delightful that you've never been to before. Something I've noticed from many years of visiting wineries, is that wines from a single vineyard smell like the earth they come from. That makes a tasting a way to sensorily visit the place where they were made.

When you're tasting with friends and family the scents and flavors you encounter can open pathways that help you connect with each other in both unique and familiar ways. It's that complex mix of new flavors, colors and the emotions they elicit that makes wine tasting exhilarating and exhausting.

As tour guides, we know that our guests are immersed in that experience when they stop taking photos, because so much of their bandwidth is consumed with the scent, the flavors and the emotional places those are taking them. We know that guests have been swept up by the joy of the tasting experience when *they start singing in the car.* It doesn't happen all the time, but it's great when it does!

Chapter Twenty
Wine Tasting with the Stars

When we first came to the North Bay, we visited the Imagery Winery in Sonoma Valley to see their remarkable collection of wine bottle art. At the time it was owned by the Benziger family, and while their other winery was bigger, Imagery was where they produced small lots of unusual grapes. The winemaker, Joe Benziger, told us the story about how they decided to commission pieces for wine labels, paying artists with ten cases of whatever wine their labels adorned.

The collection's theme is the front of the Parthenon, because there is a small, similarly proportioned white 'gazebo' that overlooks the Benziger Vineyards in Glen Ellen. It was built by the previous owner, who was a physician who grew cannabis. He would sit up there with his customers, to enjoy the wonderful view while they *sampled his wares*. Not long after newlyweds Mike and Mary Benziger drove across the country from Long Island, they bought the property. It had been farmed since the 1800's and there were still buildings there from that time. Eventually more of their family joined them in the business. Thinking back, our connections with the Benziger family and their work was a big part of what convinced us to move from Philadelphia to Sonoma, and it wasn't just about the art.

Originally, Mike farmed the land conventionally, when they had a problem with the vines, they called the chemical guy who came and sprayed the vines. Many years later during an interview for our TV show 'Wine Country at Work,' Chris Benziger, his youngest brother, told me about the day he experienced his *epiphany*. He walked outside the winery one morning and realized that standing there in the vineyard, he didn't hear any sounds from birds, insects or animals. Realizing how much the chemicals had damaged their surroundings, they started looking at growing organically, but it was Mike who became fascinated with Biodynamic farming.

He found a *book on the subject and carried it with him constantly*. They found a local consultant on Biodynamics and gradually converted the vineyards, in the process becoming Sonoma's greatest advocates for this remarkable approach. Today the ranch is vibrantly healthy, sheep graze among the vines, owls keep the gophers down, hawks keep the starlings away, circles of wild turkeys visit, and beneficial insects thrive thanks to the insectarium filled with plants that support them. Many years later when the family sold the winery, Mike shifted his attention to his local restaurant garden, and producing some of Sonoma's finest natural cannabis products. Once a farmer always a farmer!

So, what is *Biodynamics*? It is the first modern organic agriculture system started in Europe in the 1920's in response to toxic chemicals invading family farms. Up until the twentieth century all farming was organic, but after the first oil wells were drilled in the late 1860's, chemists began transforming those hydrocarbons into numerous products for fueling vehicles, lubricating machinery, creating explosives and even making pharmaceuticals. World War I was a *petrochemical* fueled war, but when Armistice Day arrived, those companies had warehouses *filled* with raw ingredients, so they repurposed them for agriculture and sanitation.

Today, of course, oil based plastics are widely used for food packaging. In a century and a half, humanity has accumulated so much discarded plastic that there is an island of it floating in the Pacific Ocean the size of Alaska. As WWI veterans returned to their farms, the companies that made tanks and trucks sold them low-cost tractors to replace oxen for plowing. That created a market for diesel fuel. They also produced chemical fertilizers and insecticides for the vineyards that they would need to buy every year, along with *chlorine* soaps to clean the wooden wine presses and tanks.

Are you wondering why the farmers didn't stick to their traditional methods instead of adopting the new technologies? Answering that requires some historical context. Traditionally farms are operated by *three* generations. The middle generation handles the management and the lion's share of the work. The younger generation helps out in between their time-consuming process of looking for a mate.

The older generation isn't working full time, but they aren't quite retired either. That's because they often lend a hand, opening a gate for the sheep at the right time, or steadying a ladder. *But the elders are also the keepers of each farm's wisdom.* They pass on the essential lore of the land to the next generation; how to recognize the signs of an early Winter from when frost first appears on the hills, or if a dangerous predator is stalking the herds from markings in the grass. They remember all the steps and recipes that a farm needs to thrive, and by recalling the past they ensure the family's future.

During the war, a significant segment of the men in the younger and middle generations from France, Germany and their allies perished, and even more were wounded. On the home front *more civilians died* than soldiers, including that older generation who struggled to run farms, while marauding armies raided their stored grains, vegetables and animals. The farming traditions, developed over thousands of years, were *disrupted* and there was a labor shortage. The modern products and time-saving solutions they were being offered seemed like life savers.

However over time, not everyone was content with this new paradigm because soldiers returning to the farm recognized those chemicals from the smells they encountered on the battlefield. When their families began developing the same symptoms they saw during the war, *they knew why*. The distinctive odor of the new chlorine soap they used on their presses and tanks smelled just like the mustard gas that scarred their lungs and killed their comrades.

There were still people here and there who remembered parts of the traditional techniques, but they needed to find someone to assemble the disparate pieces into a system they could follow. The person they found to lead the effort was Rudolph Steiner, a trained architect from Austria who made his fame as an esoteric researcher, philosopher and author. Considering that he was not a farmer, he might have seemed like an *odd choice* to lead the charge against chemical agriculture. In the end, he was the *perfect* person to do that, because he understood the underlying Hermetic philosophy that guided so many of these ancient techniques.

After generations of chemical agriculture, many of these techniques seem mystical to us today, but they were developed when farmhouses didn't have electricity, and people closely followed the *cycles of the sky* and seasons. They perceived subtle energies that most people miss today, and their language was filled with words that referred to planetary archetypes, like having a mercurial wit, or a martial personality. Rudolf conducted interviews and corresponded with elderly farmers, herbalists and astrologers. Then he organized the knowledge into a comprehensive system that he presented in a series of twenty lectures. Today he would be on *YouTube!*

Over the next hundred years, practitioners with specialized interests have fine-tuned the system. Vintners brought the knowledge from the vineyard into the winery, herbalists selected the best plants for treating the vines *homeopathically*, astrologers created *calendars* to time the many tasks, and we've even made our own small contribution to the art.

When I tell people about some of the methods, they often roll their eyes. Here is the best one! Farmers bury *cow horns* filled with ground crystal in the vineyard at the Winter Solstice. They dig them up at the Spring Equinox and mix the powdered crystal with water, to spray on the vines to help the leaves absorb sunshine. At the other seasons they fill the horns with manure that they later mix into compost that they apply to the Winter vines.

Why cow horns? There is something special about their shape that connects them to the sacred geometry of the Earth, and when they've used other containers, they don't work as well.

They time the tasks in the vineyard and the cellar by the movements of the planets, with a special preference for the positions of the Moon and Mars, and of course they follow the Lunar phases. It seems incredible that modern farmers would depend on these 'mystical' techniques, but then they see that the Biodynamic vines are healthier and, in blind tastings, the wines taste better. Many of the world's most respected wineries employ this method and the number adopting Biodynamics is growing annually.

So, what is our little contribution to Biodynamics? Let me explain that we are experienced Astrologers, Herbalists and Feng Shui consultants, an unusual collection of skills but it keeps us busy. If you do a quick online search it will turn up our many related books. Not surprisingly we found Biodynamics *fascinating*, but we were into the sixth edition of our tour books before we learned that prestigious European wineries timed their commercial tastings by the Sign of the Moon.

Now, timing agricultural tasks by the Moon's phase is an ancient practice, but timing the wine tastings, that's new! The wineries like to pour wines for their salespeople and distributors on days when the Moon is in one of the three *Fire* Signs. In Biodynamics they call those the *Fruit* Moons. They like those days because the wines open more quickly, and the fruit flavors are prominent, so they make a better first impression on their palates.

Because I often attend wine tastings, I've noticed that some days the wines are more fragrant than others, but I hadn't correlated that to the Moon's Sign. But when I looked for this connection, it was obvious. My early career as a *perfumer* gave me a well-trained nose which has been helpful working in Wine Country. But as I observed the way the wines reacted on different days, and how that affected the taster's experience, I noticed that while all the Fruit Moons had qualities in common, they were different from each other. This was also true for the three Root Moons (Earth), the three Flower Moons (Air) and the three Leaf (Water) Moons.

During a wine tasting the Fruit and Flower Moons move the energy up, so the scent reaches the nose easily. Our initial experience of wine is mostly through the *scent*, rather than the flavor. The Root and Leaf Moons move the energy down towards the ground, so the aerating flavors cling to the juice. On those days you get the best results by putting your nose inside the almost horizontal glass, just above the liquid, and below the alcohol fumes. Your nose might get wet, but you'll be able to smell the wine's bouquet.

When the wineries developed this preference for the Fruit and Flower Moons for events while avoiding the Root and Leaf Moons, it created an *unintended* consequence. In Biodynamic tasting rooms around the world the staff began to believe that the Moon was working against them half of the time. But many tasting rooms are open seven days a week. How do you deal with that? Should you only open up for tastings on good Moon days? That's not very practical, especially considering that not all Fruit and Flower Moons are equally good, nor are the Root and Leaf Moons equally bad.

To quote Shakespeare's Hamlet, "There is more things in heaven and earth, Horatio, than are dreamt of in your philosophy."

I've attended thousands of tastings and watched the purchase of millions of dollars of wine, so I can testify that every day is good for wine tasting. It's true that as the Moon changes Sign, the wines react differently.

Interestingly, as the Moon changes Sign, the type of experience clients desire also changes. Some days they want a fast tasting, and on others it's hard to get them out the door for the next appointment. On certain Moons they are hungry for education, and on others they want to educate the host. Then on the Root Days they'll ask if there is a food pairing, because it enhances the wine's flavors so much.

Learning how to manage those changing conditions is the key to producing great tasting experiences every time. I've known experienced professionals who automatically *adjusted their presentations,* even though they had no idea of the Moon's position. What they did have was plenty of life experience adjusting to change, and of course, customers. For the younger, less experienced hosts this was challenging. But we realized this knowledge might be helpful for them because post-pandemic, the tasting room staff are now mostly in their twenties and thirties.

Fortunately, that generation are *fans* of astrology, and they are grateful for these insights based on the Moon Sign, feeling that offers additional credibility. When it produces good results in the clients experience and wine sales, I know that I'm always going to be welcomed with a big smile when I return to their tasting room.

Now since we write books it is only natural that we would put these insights into one. The first version was called, 'Wine Tasting with the Stars' and it included a tasting calendar for 2023. The next year we simplified the calendar to make it easier and quicker to use, and we published the '2024 Astrology Wine Tasting Calendar and Day Planner', turning it into an annual project. Then for the 2025 edition we rebranded it as the Lunar Food and Wine Tasting Calendar, because that's what it is!

The calendar includes numerous chapters that explain the connections between the planets and wine and how to best use the information in a tasting. Yes, it's published for a ridiculously small, niche market, but whenever we put the calendar in someone's hand, they invariably *smile*, and often *laugh*, because it is such a *joyful* approach to understanding astrology and wine at the same time.

Abbot's Passage Winery

Chapter Twenty One
Tour Guides, The Funniest Business

Over the years we have run many businesses, from ridiculously small to quite large. We've worked with both individual clients and Fortune 500 companies. Without a doubt, the wine tour business is the funniest with which we've ever been involved. That's saying something, because one of our long-time businesses is as consulting astrologers and feng shui practitioners. To give you an idea of how *funny that is*, over the years those clients have included seven professional clowns and mimes, mixed in with a respectable number of millionaires and some bordering on billionaires. And even from that perspective, the wine tour business is funnier!

Let's start with the basic premise; we are driving people around various valleys filled with wineries that are just waiting for guests who want to sample their inebriating wares. Those guests will become increasingly intoxicated during the day, so that the people who climb in our vehicle in the morning may have little resemblance to those who step out of the car at the end of the day. Of course, *saying they 'step out' does not do the experience justice,* since there is a reason that I have to occasionally station myself strategically to catch them if necessary. There is a bonus though; even those people who start the day with the residual stress of traveling, invariably return to the car after the first tasting feeling so much better.

When clients first contact us, they talk with Lahni, who has a talent for putting people at ease as they plan the complexities of their visit. People like her so much that many times, when I pick up clients at their hotel they'll ask, *"Isn't Lahni coming?"* Sometimes clients are a little wary when they meet me. If they knew that this area has twice the average D.U.I. rate, and I figure that on some days one third of the drivers are drinking, they'd be even more nervous.

Luckily the first rule of wine tour driving is to be hyper-defensive. They may wonder if we have an agenda, bringing people to wineries where we have a 'special' arrangement? That's common in the travel and tour business, but that doesn't suit our needs. Our tour work is an essential part of our research for our books, so limiting ourselves to a small list of places doesn't work for us.

Also, there are too many kinds of people and too many kinds of wineries to restrict our list. Matchmaking between the clients and the wineries is an art. Successfully finding the common ground between the host and the guests makes all the difference in the winery experience.

Visitors often arrive thinking that these world-famous wine regions are filled with experts who only discuss food and wine, and that their own wine preferences and previous experiences are going to be ridiculed. This is the fault of restaurant sommeliers and amazingly *uninformative wine lists.* But that's the restaurant world, this is Wine Country. Here our guests enter the culture of growers and vintners who view themselves as farmers who produce food and beverages.

The tasting room is less related to a fancy restaurant or bar, and more like a very stylish fruit stand, with their best fruit ready for tasting and sale. The juice that didn't make the grade goes out the back door as *bulk wine,* and if they really screwed it up, which happens, it's off to the ethanol plant. The thing that matters most is the guests' preferences, what they like and dislike. Or as hosts often say, "The best wine is the one you like!"

As we cruise up into the valleys in our big SUV, my first job is to put them at ease. I do that by focusing on their interests and explaining what makes the region special. I spend a little time talking about the wines they prefer, and about the type of vines we see out the windows. Many grape varieties prefer specific types of geology and climate, so when you go through an area, the vineyards are usually two of three related types.

Which is good, because while I can sometimes tell a varietal by the leaf shape, I really like it when they have a *little sign* at the end of the row. While clients will tell me the wines they like, getting down to the guests' true wine preferences is the job of the winery hosts. That's because people's palates often go through a transformation during a series of tastings where the grapes were grown, and the wines were made.

The *only time* I focus on wine is during a quick tutorial I do, usually at the first winery, on tasting like a professional. Most people know how to enjoy wine, pour it from the bottle to a glass, take a sip or three and repeat. But many first-time visitors never learned to use the glass properly to 'taste' wines. That's because they normally have wine as an accompaniment to a meal, not as the main event.

If you've never sat through a tasting session, we suggest you watch some videos about wine tasting. These simple techniques are not complicated, but they do help your senses of scent and taste work more effectively, so you can completely experience the wine and increase your enjoyment. The swirling, sniffing and holding the glass at an angle so you can rest your nose on the inside of the bottom lip may seem pretentious, but it is the best way to capture the various components of the wine. The swirling helps the wines to open up by mixing it with oxygen so it can be inhaled by your nose. Holding the glass at an angle and placing your nose at the lower lip allows the alcohol fumes, which can mask the wine's aroma, to flow out the top of the glass.

Meanwhile your *nose*, held just above the liquid, is able to experience the wine's pleasing, unmasked fruit scents. The nose detects an amazing number of fragrances, and it tells the body all about the wine. That also gives your digestive system a heads up to start producing the enzymes necessary to digest it. Once you sip the wine, before you swallow, you slowly swirl it around your mouth, so that it touches the various tastebuds long enough to make an impression.

This process is outside most people's daily experience because most of us don't ask our senses of smell and taste to do very much. We eat the same favorite, familiar foods and beverages day in and day out! The tasting room is a place where guests can allow their senses to experience the wine without any distractions. They can taste numerous wines side by side which expands their library of flavors and changes the way they experience wine from then on.

People who work in the tasting room become accustomed to focusing on *scent and flavor*, often at the expense of their other faculties. I remember one of the hosts saying, "I realized I was a wine geek when I started swirling my orange juice at breakfast!" Once people realize the difference that these techniques make in the experience of the wines, they'll do it that way for the rest of the day.

Part of a guide's work is managing the emotions of the day, like the way a mother manages the emotions of her family by how she arranges the furniture, and what she chooses to cook for them. That's because flavor, emotions and spatial memory live in the same part of the brain, so just like you never forget how a person makes you feel, you never forget a flavor or a scent. This is connected to how we recall locations, so whenever you taste that wine in the future, it will bring you back to the place where you first experienced it. Many times, clients say that they want to return to wineries that they've visited before where they had a very emotionally enjoyable visit. They'll praise the host by name, and that often plays a bigger part than the quality of the wines.

During my early years of touring, most wineries had bar tastings that rarely required an appointment. Most of the tasting room hosts were part time, so it was hit or miss about how much they could share with the guest. I typically went inside with my guests and observed. I've visited certain wineries so many times that I became more familiar with the wines and the *winery's story* than the hosts, so I would illuminate those topics for my guests because people forget facts, but they remember stories and flavors. Of course, if a host sounded knowledgeable, I would sit in the back and listen to the presentation, and hopefully hear some new stories, as they poured the various wines.

That type of casual eavesdropping helped me plan the rest of tour. Often for the first winery I chose one that offered a wide variety of wines so I could accurately gauge their palates. Many times, what clients told us about their preferences during our pre-tour phone calls turned out to be quite different from the wines they eventually shipped home.

At its core, the wine tour business is about transportation, so a great deal of thought goes into what the tour companies drive. Early in our research for our first book Ralph drove for a local company in *low, sleek black limousines,* the rare SUV and the occasional bus. The classic black limo is more suited to cruising around city streets than on country roads and they always seem horribly out of place in wine country. Girls in short dresses struggle, often unsuccessfully, to climb out of those low limos with their modesty intact. Their visibility is poor for both the passengers and the driver, and the black exteriors turn them into *heat* sinks that strain the air conditioning on hot days.

We were the first company to use a silver SUV for our tours, and since then they've become increasingly popular. Most of the Wine Country companies have abandoned stretch limos for SUV's and tall Sprinters, which are easier to get into and out of gracefully. For us, the limo's biggest failing was the tiny window that connected the driver to the passengers, making any kind of informative conversation painfully difficult.

Admittedly, the guest could close that window for a little privacy, which is a popular tactic on prom nights. But, on a wine tour, it makes it hard for the driver to monitor how inebriated the clients become. This was made *worse* by the company's policy of stocking the car with a bottle of cheap sparkling wine and glasses. So, they started the day feeling encouraged to overdo the drinking. I've lost count of the number of times people had to be poured out of the limos at the end of the day.

The big, *luxury* SUVs were an excellent improvement because the passengers all faced forward and they had a better view of these beautiful vineyards and architecture. Someone told us that in New England, big SUVs are called "Moose Mobiles," because you could hit a moose in one and still survive. No one talked about how the moose felt about that encounter.

Considering that the work requires driving in an area where up to thirty percent of the drivers have been drinking, and the area has *twice* the DUI rate of the rest of the state, having a big muscular car makes good sense. It's also the reason guides go through a great deal of coffee during the day, you always have to be on your toes.

Over the years, as the wines and the tasting experiences became more expensive, spending the day in Napa or Sonoma as a kind of cheap *'booze cruise'* mostly fell out of fashion. With the average tasting fees at each winery being the price of a nice meal, you want to remember where you went, and not have the entire day turn into a wine-colored haze.

We've seen interesting cycles in the business. For instance, the number of out of state visitors usually drops in the first year of a new Presidential administration. During a previous administration that was particularly unfriendly to foreigners, our international visitors practically disappeared and that market was slow to recover. We especially noticed this because we work in five languages, at varying levels of fluency, which guarantees us a certain number of international customers annually.

The Wine Tour season starts in April and goes on through November. That is coincidentally the *growing* cycle of the grape vines. Bud break begins in March and April, and by the end of November all the grapes are off the vines and in the tanks. July is typically a quiet month. Why? Because it is a popular time for family events.

Just as significantly, our visitors tend to be well traveled and if they are going to France or Italy in the Summer, they prefer July because those countries shut down in August for their own vacations. During COVID, when people could travel to Europe only with great difficulty, Wine Country was busy in July. If travelers can't go to Europe's Wine Country, they come here and they don't need a passport or to brush up on their French. In 2023 Europe finally opened and their hotel bookings were up by forty percent,while the bookings in the North Bay were down by the same percentage.

There are so many enjoyable parts to the wine tour business. We visit beautiful places and meet remarkable people from all over the world. Not surprisingly our wine cellars are overflowing and the folks at the wineries love to *feed* us. This area has more wine educators than any place else on the planet, so if you sit in the back of the room and listen, you can learn a great deal about wine, history and culture.

Because our clients are educated, well-traveled and often wine aficionados, we learn a tremendous amount from them. One of the most interesting aspects has been our friendships with the other guides. Within the hospitality world the independent guides are a small community of very colorful, resourceful and entertaining people. They come from *diverse* backgrounds and parts of the world. Many ran successful businesses before this one and happened upon this work in a casual way, just to find that they were good at it, and they enjoyed this unique profession.

You really know you have found a *'home'* when you have a lull in the tour work, and you immediately miss those days on the road, visiting your friends at the wineries and your soon to be new friends, your guests. Besides, where else would we hear these delightful stories and then find guests we can tell them to? Thank you for listening!

Chapter Twenty Two
Afterthought, the Fans

Move To a Vineyard, It Will Be Romantic...!

As we said, we got into the winery tour
business quite by accident. We had attended a conference in San Francisco 18 months before and stayed on
for a sorely needed vacation. The idea of writing a book
about winery buildings from a Feng Shui perspective was
the project that inspired us to move 3,000 miles from
Philadelphia to Wine Country. It had only taken us 18
months to wrap up the ongoing certification classes we
were teaching and figure out the logistics of this coast-to-
coast move. Once we settled in, we started our research.
It was a fun process because we were, after all, in Wine

Country, and we already had a great deal of interest, and a little knowledge about wine. As we made personal connections with a few winemakers and winery owners, our 'buildings book' idea took shape.

We *first* moved to Sonoma for our research and Ralph was out every few days visiting wineries, meeting key people, photographing buildings and developing content. Winery people are a chatty bunch, and they love the idea of inspiring a book. In addition to winemakers and owners, he ran into more than a few tour guides. Then he got the brilliant idea to take a part time job driving wine tours. Why not get paid for a little on-the-job research?

This smart move got him *up close and personal* at a huge number of wineries, talking to people who were grateful for the customers he brought. In the course of his interviews, a secondary theme began to evolve. These winery folks were asking for a 'connect-the-dots' type of tour book to answer visitors' questions about where to eat, where to stay, which winery would they recommend and more. Now, Ralph has a great feel for sales and can't ignore the interests of the 'marketplace.'

As the 'building book' *morphed* into a tour book, we became more and more connected with hotels and wineries, especially in Napa. When opportunities opened up there, we realized it was time to move closer to our connections. Friends suggested different areas and options in Napa, and all of them were very close to the vineyards, something we did not have nearby in Sonoma.

How cool would that be? Living a stone's throw from the wineries that Ralph was visiting with his guests.

"Move to a vineyard," they said. *"It will be romantic,"* they said. After an extensive search, we moved in July and found an idyllic spot near the Oak Knoll AVA with beautiful vineyards and wineries a block away. Perfect...!

Fast forward to a Winter night in late March, cozy in our bed at 3AM, when suddenly we hear what could only be a *'bevy of helicopters'* hunting down a crime suspect in our quiet little part of paradise. We say 'bevy' because we were used to the occasional copter in the middle of the night due to being close to a hospital with an emergency helipad. "What is going on?" The sound sort of came and went, like waves of aircraft heading to the west. Could they be squadrons from Travis Air Force Base? If so, something big was happening.

"Turn on the air cleaner... where are my ear plugs... no, throw on some clothes, we have to go out and get to the *bottom* of this." By this time, it was 5 am. "I'll buy you a Starbucks! We have to see what's going on."

If you have been to Wine Country, you may have noticed those big fan-looking things in the middle of some vineyards. We encountered them in Sonoma and when we asked, they said, "Oh, those are frost fans, but they aren't really used anymore." Well, maybe not in Sonoma but they are everywhere in frostier Napa. And when overnight temps get close to freezing around the time of bud break, they certainly use them. Wineries will not let a whole vineyard of expensive Cabernet vines freeze-dry before they can make their expensive wine. The noisy motors are droning enough, but they also oscillate, adding to that whirring sound that left our brains buzzing.

You know how people have that pet that destroys everything, or yips incessantly and you often wonder, 'Why do they keep that pet?" Well, we understand why now, because we still live in paradise in ear shot of the fans, and we know where they keep the ear plugs at the local Orchard Supply store. And now we know why they carry so many.

We hope you enjoy this book as much as we have enjoyed writing it. And come visit us out here in Wine Country!

Acknowledgements

As we gathered stories over twenty years many people contributed to them. Some stories go back generations, being passed down through families, friends and winery employees. Over the years the stories changed in the telling, sometimes getting more entertaining, but other times straying from the truth. So, we've done deep research to keep the stories mostly authentic, while doing our best to tap into the passion that fuels so many of them. We thank those generations of storytellers who cared enough to share these tales.

Some of these chapters are not stories, but rather an insider's glimpse at the world of grapes, wine, and tasting room hospitality. Surely other people are more expert in these fields and have their own opinions, but we have endeavored to present a clear picture from our perspective as tour guides.

We thank the countless winery hosts, including a significant number of owners and winemakers, who have shared their knowledge with us during thousands of wine tastings and tours. Certain people have been especially generous with their knowledge, Chris Loxton of Loxton Cellars taught me so much about winemaking that I could surely make my own label. Squire Fridell of GlenLyon Vineyards taught me about the art and history of winemaking and the genius of wine salesmanship.

Thank you George Webber, historian, actor, educator, colleague and our frequent television show guest. He created so many wonderful educational programs about this region's history for Jean-Charles Boisset, who restored numerous historic buildings including the iconic Buena Vista Winery

Thank you Napa natives Susanna Kelham, who filled in so much about Napa's culture, Liz Allesio, whose stories about Napa's history provided valuable context, and Sheli Smith, who made so many resources available to us through the Napa County Historical Society.

Important parts of this book would not exist without Shelly & Marty Mochizuki's answers to our endless questions about viticulture, and their wonderful stories about working in the vineyards. Shelly was also our reader at a critical point in the project's development.

Many topflight tour guides shared stories with us as we waited for our guests including Barry Smith, with his remarkable insights about the industry, and his wife Kerry Smith, a formidable local architecture historian, which she weaves into her artwork.

Thank you all! Ralph & Lahni

About Ralph & Lahni DeAmicis

Ralph and Lahni found their way from professional speaking into writing about wine country by starting to create a book about winery buildings. One day Ralph chatted up a local tour driver who possessed a wealth of information about winery buildings, and apparently that knowledge was part of a guide's toolbox. So, Ralph got a part-time job driving tours, but as he navigated around the valleys, they realized there wasn't a good 'winery' tour book. So, in 2008 the project morphed into their first winery guidebook. In 2024 they produced their seventh edition, and the series continues to be the region's favorite.

Eventually Ralph & Lahni started their own tour company which has taken them to many beautiful places, while connecting them to the winemaking community. In 2012 they began producing 'Wine Country at Work' at Napa Valley Television, which includes both interviews and documentary films about the wine region. They continue to create books and videos and speak to groups about this wonderful place they call home.

Other Titles by The Authors

A Tour Guide's Napa Valley
A Tour Guide's Sonoma Wine Country
Sonoma Navigator, Maps & Highlights
Napa Navigator, Maps & Highlights
Napa Valley Winery Maps
Sonoma Winery Maps

PlanetaryCalendar.com
Published Annually since 1949

Planetary Calendar Astrology Forecasts & Health Hints
Two Wall Sizes, a Pocket Size, a Day Planner &
a Digital Version for your Phone and Computer
The Lunar Food and Wine Tasting Calendar
The Companion Book
'Planetary Calendar Astrology,
Moving Beyond Observation to Action'
Coming Soon
Reclaiming Astrology from the Patriarchy
The Story of the Stolen Zodiac

From the 'Tango' Series
Feng Shui and the Tango, The Dance of Design
Feng Shui and the Tango, The Essential Chapters
25th Anniversary Edition
FS&T Prosperity Lessons
FS&T Happiness Lessons
The Dream Desk Quiz
The Clutter Bug's Emergency Handbook

Find their books and documentaries at:
www.WineCountryInShorts.com

Made in the USA
Columbia, SC
10 October 2024

43419294R00154